OPPOSING
VIEWPOINTS®
SERIES

Problems with Death

Other Books of Related Interest

Opposing Viewpoints Series

Abortion

Death and Dying

The Death Penalty

Euthanasia

Homosexuality

Problems of Death

Suicide

Teens at Risk

Current Controversies Series

The Abortion Controversy

Assisted Suicide

Capital Punishment

Medical Ethics

Mental Health

Suicide

At Issue Series

Anitdepressants

The Ethics of Abortion

The Ethics of Capital Punishment

The Ethics of Euthanasia

How Should One Cope with Death?

Physician-Assisted Suicide

The Right to Die

"Congress shall make no law . . . abridging the freedom of speech, or of the press."

First Amendment to the U.S. Constitution

The basic foundation of our democracy is the First Amendment guarantee of freedom of expression. The Opposing Viewpoints Series is dedicated to the concept of this basic freedom and the idea that it is more important to practice it than to enshrine it.

OPPOSING VIEWPOINTS® SERIES

Problems with Death

David A. Becker and Cynthia S. Becker, Book Editors

GREENHAVEN PRESS

An imprint of Thomson Gale, a part of The Thomson Corporation

THOMSON

GALE

Detroit • New York • San Francisco • New Haven, Conn. • Waterville, Maine • London

LIBRARY OF CONGRESS CATALOGING-IN-PUBLICATION DATA

Problems with death / David A. Becker and Cynthia S. Becker, book editors.
p. cm. -- (Opposing viewpoints)
Includes bibliographical references and index.
ISBN 0-7377-2953-8 (lib. : alk. paper) -- ISBN 0-7377-2954-6 (pbk. : alk. paper)
1. Death--Social aspects--United States. 2. Death--Moral and ethical aspects--United States. 3. Abortion--United States. 4. Suicide--United States. 5. Capital punishment--United States. I. Becker, David A. (David Allison) II. Becker, Cynthia S. (Cynthia Simmelink) III. Opposing viewpoints series (Unnumbered)
HQ1073.5.U6P76 2007
179.7--dc22

2006041236

Printed in the United States of America
10 9 8 7 6 5 4 3 2 1

Contents

Why Consider Opposing Viewpoints?

> *"The only way in which a human being can make some approach to knowing the whole of a subject is by hearing what can be said about it by persons of every variety of opinion and studying all modes in which it can be looked at by every character of mind. No wise man ever acquired his wisdom in any mode but this."*
>
> John Stuart Mill

In our media-intensive culture it is not difficult to find differing opinions. Thousands of newspapers and magazines and dozens of radio and television talk shows resound with differing points of view. The difficulty lies in deciding which opinion to agree with and which "experts" seem the most credible. The more inundated we become with differing opinions and claims, the more essential it is to hone critical reading and thinking skills to evaluate these ideas. Opposing Viewpoints books address this problem directly by presenting stimulating debates that can be used to enhance and teach these skills. The varied opinions contained in each book examine many different aspects of a single issue. While examining these conveniently edited opposing views, readers can develop critical thinking skills such as the ability to compare and contrast authors' credibility, facts, argumentation styles, use of persuasive techniques, and other stylistic tools. In short, the Opposing Viewpoints Series is an ideal way to attain the higher-level thinking and reading skills so essential in a culture of diverse and contradictory opinions.

In addition to providing a tool for critical thinking, Opposing Viewpoints books challenge readers to question their own strongly held opinions and assumptions. Most people form their opinions on the basis of upbringing, peer pressure, and personal, cultural, or professional bias. By reading carefully balanced opposing views, readers must directly confront new ideas as well as the opinions of those with whom they disagree. This is not to simplistically argue that everyone who reads opposing views will—or should—change his or her opinion. Instead, the series enhances readers' understanding of their own views by encouraging confrontation with opposing ideas. Careful examination of others' views can lead to the readers' understanding of the logical inconsistencies in their own opinions, perspective on why they hold an opinion, and the consideration of the possibility that their opinion requires further evaluation.

Evaluating Other Opinions

To ensure that this type of examination occurs, Opposing Viewpoints books present all types of opinions. Prominent spokespeople on different sides of each issue as well as well-known professionals from many disciplines challenge the reader. An additional goal of the series is to provide a forum for other, less known, or even unpopular viewpoints. The opinion of an ordinary person who has had to make the decision to cut off life support from a terminally ill relative, for example, may be just as valuable and provide just as much insight as a medical ethicist's professional opinion. The editors have two additional purposes in including these less known views. One, the editors encourage readers to respect others' opinions—even when not enhanced by professional credibility. It is only by reading or listening to and objectively evaluating others' ideas that one can determine whether they are worthy of consideration. Two, the inclusion of such viewpoints encourages the important critical thinking skill of objectively evaluating an author's credentials and bias. This evaluation will illuminate an author's reasons for taking a particular stance on an issue and will aid in readers' evaluation of the author's ideas.

It is our hope that these books will give readers a deeper understanding of the issues debated and an appreciation of the complexity of even seemingly simple issues when good and honest people disagree. This awareness is particularly important in a democratic society such as ours in which people enter into public debate to determine the common good. Those with whom one disagrees should not be regarded as enemies but rather as people whose views deserve careful examination and may shed light on one's own.

Thomas Jefferson once said that "difference of opinion leads to inquiry, and inquiry to truth." Jefferson, a broadly educated man, argued that "if a nation expects to be ignorant and free . . . it expects what never was and never will be." As individuals and as a nation, it is imperative that we consider the opinions of others and examine them with skill and discernment. The Opposing Viewpoints Series is intended to help readers achieve this goal.

David L. Bender and Bruno Leone,
Founders

Introduction

> *"We hold these truths to be self-evident,*
> *that all men are created equal, that they*
> *are endowed by their Creator with*
> *certain inalienable Rights, that among*
> *these are Life, Liberty and the pursuit of*
> *Happiness."*
>
> *—Thomas Jefferson,*
> *the Declaration of Independence*

At the heart of American democracy is respect for the sanctity of life. Thomas Jefferson articulated this value in the Declaration of Independence when he referred to the right to life as an inalienable right. In the abstract, Americans agree that each individual's life is equally important and deserving of protection. Despite this seeming consensus, however, Americans are in fact deeply divided about the meaning of "right to life." Some people, for example, adamantly oppose abortion, suicide, and euthanasia because, in their opinion, these practices violate the sanctity of life, yet they support the death penalty as proper punishment for those who take life.

President George W. Bush personifies this dilemma. He identifies himself as pro-life. He opposes abortion, seeing it as a violation of the fetus's right to life. In a 1999 speech he summed up his position, stating, "I believe that life is valuable, even when it is unwanted, even when it is physically imperfect . . . unborn children should be welcomed in life and protected in law. This is the ideal: a generous society that values every life." Yet, the president supports capital punishment. "The reason to support the death penalty," he said during the 2000 presidential debates, "is that it saves other people's lives." Believing in the deterrent effect of capital punishment, he allowed the execution of 134 inmates while serving as governor of Texas.

President Bush is not alone in holding what could be seen as conflicting views on the sanctity of life. In a January 2006 report issued by the Pew Research Center for the People and the Press, the center notes, "Relatively few Americans subscribe to what may be termed as a consistent 'ethic of life.'" For instance, when examining people's attitudes toward abortion, capital punishment, suicide, and euthanasia, one might expect that Americans would fall into two camps: those who support all of them, and those who support none of them. However, the vast majority of Americans approve of some of these practices while vociferously opposing others. For example, the center observes that many Americans oppose both abortion and the death penalty because they kill human life, but "abortion opponents and death penalty opponents alike overwhelmingly believe that there are circumstances in which doctors and nurses should let a patient die." In fact, 60 percent of people surveyed by the Pew Research Center believe that individuals have a moral right to end their own lives if they are in great pain with no hope of improvement.

At the same time, people who favor physician-assisted suicide for the terminally ill may have strong objections to suicide in general. While some analysts believe that dying patients in irremediable pain have a right to put an end to their lives, these same people might feel that it is wrong for people suffering emotional pain to kill themselves. Many suicide opponents object to the practice because it harms the suicide's family and friends, who must live not only with the loss of their loved one but also with the guilt of not having been able to stop the death. To these critics' way of thinking, people who commit suicide are supremely selfish. These analysts also think that suicide is a permanent solution to a temporary problem, a problem that could be adequately addressed by therapy and antidepressants.

How can such contradictions over problems of death be explained? The answer appears to lie in the circumstances surrounding death. For example, guilt or innocence is often seen as a defining circumstance. To some Americans, a fetus is an innocent life, deserving of protection. In contrast, they believe, a murderer is guilty of taking an innocent life and therefore deserves to die. For these analysts, the important factor is the guilt or innocence of the life taken. Their feelings become more complicated when the issue of euthanasia is being evaluated. On the one hand, they might support euthanasia because the dying patient is obviously innocent, and society has a moral obligation to end suffering. On the other hand, these analysts might oppose euthanasia for fear that legalizing the practice will lead to a devaluation of human life in general, which will make the killing of other innocents more prevalent. In regards to suicide, many of these analysts feel that a person has a right to commit suicide because in killing themselves, they do no harm to others and are thus innocent. Conversely, suicide may be seen as an act that harms survivors, making the one taking his or her life guilty.

Conflicts over death will certainly persist within individuals and in American society. The authors in *Opposing Viewpoints: Problems with Death* examine these conflicts in the following chapters: Is Abortion Ethical? Is the Death Penalty Necessary? What Factors Contribute to Teen Suicide? Should Physician Assisted Suicide Be Condoned? Despite Jefferson's assertion that the right to life is inalienable, determining if and when life should be taken will remain highly contentious, dividing individuals within themselves, and Americans from each other.

OPPOSING
VIEWPOINTS®
SERIES

| Is Abortion Ethical?

Chapter Preface

Since the Supreme Court issued the landmark 1973 *Roe v. Wade* decision, abortion has become an intensely divisive political issue. Jan Crawford Greenburg, writing for the *Chicago Tribune* on December 28, 2005, described *Roe* as "at once, a rallying cry and a dividing line, passionately viewed as either a key protector of women's rights or a lawless exercise in judicial overreaching . . . It has become the ultimate touchstone, a ready form of shorthand, in the ongoing conflict over culture and values in America."

The divide can be seen in the 2004 platforms of the Democratic and Republican parties. The Democratic platform stated, "Because we believe in the privacy and equality of women, we stand proudly for a woman's right to choose, consistent with *Roe v. Wade*, and regardless of her ability to pay." The Republican platform opposed *Roe* stating, "The unborn child has a fundamental right to life which cannot be infringed. . . . We oppose using public revenues for abortion and will not fund organizations which advocate it. We support the appointment of judges who respect traditional family values and the sanctity of innocent human life."

Politicians' stance on abortion can have significant implications. Some analysts believe that John Kerry, the 2004 Democratic presidential candidate, lost the election in part due to his party's pro-choice position. In a May 1, 2005, article for *USA Today*, journalist Susan Page reported that a postelection survey by Stan Greenberg found that "the abortion issue was a significant factor in Kerry's loss of white Catholic voters." The Catholic Church even proposed to excommunicate politicians who support abortion.

Following its 2004 election losses, the Democratic Party and many of its most prominent members sought to find a middle ground to win over conservative Democrats and Republican voters. In a January 24, 2005, address to the Family Planning Advocates of New York State, Democratic senator Hillary Clinton called on both sides of the reproductive rights issue to find "common ground." In what many considered a direct appeal to anti-abortion voters, Clinton said, "I for one respect those who believe with all their hearts and conscience that there are no circumstances under which abortion should be available." She went on to join forces with anti-abortion Democrats in support of legislation to fund contraceptives and family planning for poor women and sex education for teenagers.

The Supreme Court itself has felt the continuing impact of *Roe v. Wade*. With the death of Chief Justice William Rehnquist and the resignation of Associate Justice Sandra Day O'Connor, the pro and anti-abortion factions saw the opportunity to shape future decisions of the Court. Abortion became the primary focus of Senate hearings on the nominees. Both sides attempted to extract some statement from each candidate that might predict how he would vote on future abortion-related cases. Republicans, who in 2005 controlled both the House and the Senate, as well as the White House, ultimately prevailed. Conservative nominee John Roberts was confirmed with relative ease as the new chief justice. Samuel A. Alito, considered to be even more conservative by some, faced more opposition than Roberts but was ultimately confirmed.

Since *Roe v. Wade*, presidents, congressional representatives, and judges are often evaluated based on their position on abortion. Political parties win or lose elections due to their stance on this most contentious issue. The politics of abortion illustrate just how strongly Americans feel about the issue. Authors in the following chapter continue the debate, exploring how abortion affects women, children, and society.

"A woman deciding whether to continue
a pregnancy stands on moral ground.
She is entitled to make her decision.
... No one else ... should decide
whether she will use her body to bring
new life into the world."

Abortion Is Ethical

Caitlin Borgmann

In the following viewpoint Caitlin Borgmann argues that abortion is ethical for many reasons. First, women have the right to decide what to do with their own bodies, she contends. Second, abortion allows women to participate equally in society by enabling them to postpone childbearing until they finish school or establish their careers. Borgmann also maintains that abortion allows women to have children only when they are ready to take care of them, and protects their health by allowing women to terminate pregnancies at legal clinics. At the time this article was written, Caitlin Borgmann was state strategies coordinator for the American Civil Liberties Union Reproductive Freedom Project in New York.

As you read, consider the following questions:

1. What two groups of women does the author suggest suffer the most due to restrictions on abortion rights?
2. In the author's view, in addition to a woman's right to choose, what else does the pro-choice movement stand for?
3. What examples does the author use to support her argument that institutional opposition to abortion rights is part of a campaign to undermine women's autonomy and equality?

The movement to preserve and advance reproductive freedom is suffering the consequences of a great victory. The establishment of the constitutional right to abortion in *Roe v. Wade* was a monumental step that changed the lives of American women. Girls grow up today under the mantle of *Roe*, never having known a world in which illegal, unsafe, degrading and sometimes fatal abortions were the norm. That is a cause for celebration as *Roe* turns 30. It is also, however, a cause of complacency. Movements typically subside after winning major legal or political battles, and ours has not escaped this cycle.

Complacency corrodes all freedoms. It is particularly dangerous to reproductive freedom because our opponents are single-minded and fervent to the point of fanaticism. Their crusade has fueled three decades of incremental restrictions that make it risky or burdensome to get an abortion and, for some women, block access altogether. Understandably, the pro–choice movement has grown frustrated with the unending onslaught, and the public, numb. The movement's responses to this conundrum have varied over time and among its many spokespersons. Yet, two recurring approaches—to jolt the public by forecasting *Roe*'s reversal and to court reluctant supporters by steering wide of abortion altogether—are problematic. We need to recapture at least some of the moral urgency that led to *Roe*, and we must meet the assaults head-on.

Reproductive freedom is in trouble. The Supreme Court has refrained from overturning *Roe* but has allowed the states to layer myriad restrictions on abortion. The states, seizing the opportunity to regulate women's lives, enacted more than 300 restrictions on access to abortion and other reproductive health services between 1995 and 2001. Some of the most common laws affect all women seeking abortions in a particular state: For example, 18 states require counseling designed to dissuade women from having abortions, followed by a waiting period before an abortion can be performed.

Low-Income Women and Teenagers Suffer Abortion Restrictions

The assault on *Roe* has done the most damage, however, to women whose voices are largely ignored in the political debate and whose interests carry the least political weight. Low-income women face what can be prohibitive costs in seeking abortions. Very few have private health insurance, and government-supported plans rarely pay for abortions. Moreover, these women face significant financial obstacles merely to get to a provider. Nationwide, 87% of all counties lack abortion providers (because of inadequate training opportunities for medical students, burdensome regulations targeted at abortion providers, and a climate of harassment and violence, among other factors). For low-income women living in rural areas, this can mean adding costs for travel, time away from jobs and child care to the cost of the abortion itself.

Teenagers have also suffered the brunt of abortion restrictions. More than half the states enforce laws that deny those younger than 18 access to a legal abortion unless they involve a parent or go to court. Teenagers who consult their parents under compulsion of the law and against their better judgment often find their fears justified: They are kicked out of their homes, beaten and prevented from obtaining abortions. The alternative of going to court is daunting for any teenager, and especially for one who is pregnant, desperate and unsupported by her family. Often, she must explain multiple absences from school without raising suspicions, find a lawyer who will help her, brave one or more trips to the courthouse, tell the intimate details of her personal life to numerous strangers and then hope that the judge grants her the permission she needs.

Yet, advocates for reproductive freedom tire of talking about these restrictions, and few people seem interested in hearing about them. Because most middle-class, adult women can get abortions in spite of the prevalent restrictions, the majoritarian passion to preserve the right established in *Roe* has faded, leaving the most vulnerable women isolated and powerless. They have reason to wonder what we are celebrating at *Roe*'s anniversary.

What we need to celebrate is renewed unity, comment, energy and purpose. Unfortunately, the movement has sometimes tried to achieve these by either dwelling on the possibility that abortion will again be illegal or minimizing the importance of abortion. We refer to these two tendencies as the apocalyptic and the apologetic approaches.

The Apocalyptic Approach

The apocalyptic approach aims to rouse the public from complacency by positing an immediate and personal threat: Women will no longer be able to get an abortion when they need one. This approach recognizes that a woman who thinks that the abortion rights battle is over and won can be goaded into action if she is convinced that the victory is about to be reversed and that its reversal will affect her. The threat posed must be imminent, real and personal.

Typically, the apocalyptic approach warns that the Supreme Court is on the brink of overturning *Roe v. Wade*. To emphasize the immediacy of the threat, this approach highlights the hostility of the current administration [that of George W. Bush] and the advancing age of several justices who support women's right to choose [in fact, Sandra Day O'Connor resigned in July and William Rehnquist died in September 2005]. Focusing on the worst-case scenario—the Court's complete overturning of *Roe*—makes the threat personal to a broad swath of Americans. Thus, this approach hopes to draw in people who are not moved to activism in opposition to narrower restrictions.

There can be no doubt that the already battered right declared in *Roe* faces new and powerful assaults. Both the White House and the Congress are enemies of choice and stand prepared to appoint and confirm like-minded judges— not only to the Supreme Court, but also to the lower federal courts where most abortion rights cases are derided. In addition, Congress is now in a position to pass long-threatened federal restrictions, posing yet more obstacles to abortion nationwide.

Courts Will Continue to Restrict Roe

The question remains, however, whether these assaults will prove fatal to *Roe* itself. If history is any guide, the Supreme Court may well continue to say that *Roe* is good law while upholding one restriction after another. This is the compromise the Court adopted in the late 1980s and openly embraced in its 1992 decision in *Planned Parenthood v. Casey*. The Court there proclaimed, "the essential holding of *Roe v. Wade* should be retained and once again reaffirmed," but then added, "the fact that a law . . . has the incidental effect of making it more difficult or more expensive to procure an abortion cannot be enough to invalidate it." If the Court follows this pattern, the damage, while devastating, will continue to be incremental, cumulative and obscure, rather than dramatic, sudden and obvious. Of course, the harms will accumulate faster as the courts grow more hostile.

Because a candid reversal of *Roe* is neither certain nor immediate, people may react to constant warnings as they would to a car alarm that goes off at all hours—it is annoying, but they learn to ignore it. We risk being unable to galvanize the public if and when we confront the imminent possibility of Roe's demise.

Moreover, constantly referring to the possibility of losing, the "core right" to abortion diverts attention from the significant encroachments that have already been and continue to be placed on the right. Under this approach, whether the core right exists is effectively measured by whether a middle-class, adult woman has access to an abortion. Meanwhile, a low-income woman has, for all intents and purposes, already lost her core right if she depends on Medicaid for her medical care but is denied coverage for an abortion; if she lives in a rural state with no abortion provider within 200 miles; and if she must make two trips to that distant provider, thanks to a state-imposed waiting period. Her right is a hollow promise when the government is permitted to erect so many hurdles that they create an impasse.

The Apologetic Approach

The apologetic approach takes a different tack. Reacting to a widespread and apparently growing discomfort with abortion, it focuses predominantly on topics the public finds more palatable, such as contraception and sexuality education. It minimizes discussion of abortion, or characterizes abortion as regrettably necessary.

This approach hopes to garner additional supporters for the movement's overall agenda by beginning with more popular subjects. Unfortunately, it does not always proceed from there. Bringing people into the fold by first discussing different (though related) issues may create an opening to convince them about the importance of access to abortion, but it is not a substitute.

The apologetic approach also hopes to draw people in by identifying with their misgivings about abortion. Respect for uncertainties and objections is critical to any conversation about deeply held values, but the apologetic approach does not engage in moral dialogue. Instead, it mirrors the public's general skittishness about abortion.

The tendency to shy from open discussion of and support for abortion plays into the hands of our opponents. They want the public to associate abortion with secrecy, trauma, stigma, guilt, fear and shame. Both our silence and our apologies reinforce these associations, however unintentionally. Our opponents say that abortion is murder, we imply or say that it is regrettable, and the public slides further into ambivalence. Recent polling data suggest such slippage in public support.

Furthermore, the apologetic approach tacitly promotes the myth that the pro–choice movement is too extreme. This approach calls for putting on a fresh and friendly face, to contrast with the glare of the stereotypical radical feminist. But we have not been frowning on childbearing, fighting for abortion on demand until moments before birth or generally scorning the views of the public. We do not need to pursue moderation as though we have been guilty of extremism.

Pro-Choice Is About More than Abortion

When we smile brightly and sidestep the issue of abortion, we risk alienating our strongest supporters. They understand that abortion rights are part of a larger constellation of both rights and aspirations. We stand not only for the right to choose, but also for comprehensive sexuality education, effective contraceptive options, quality prenatal care and childbirth assistance, and trustworthy and affordable child care. Focusing on abortion to the exclusion of all else is a mistake—but so is avoiding the subject of abortion. When we are evasive, our supporters may doubt our commitment, even if they understand that our evasiveness reflects a tactical strategy rather than a shift in principle. They may wonder about the effectiveness of outreach efforts that omit or equivocate about so important a topic and, thus, forgo the opportunity to educate people about the ongoing, cumulative damage to abortion rights.

In its hesitance to defend abortion, the apologetic approach shrinks from the wrong demon. It is an unwanted or unhealthy pregnancy that causes a woman to confront the abortion decision. Once she is in this predicament, abortion may be a welcome solution among very limited options. Bemoaning abortion is like lamenting open-heart surgery in the face of Americans' unacceptably high rate of heart disease. We hope never to need a coronary bypass, but we are grateful to have the procedure available if we need it. Similarly, as critics of the apologetic approach have pointed out, "One can feel bad, sorry, or regretful that any woman ever has an unwanted pregnancy. One can also feel truly wonderful that safe abortions are legally available when wanted." These are not contradictory positions.

Abortion as a Moral Choice

An alternative to the apocalyptic and apologetic approaches is a realistic, direct defense that recalls the reasons we fought for legal abortion in the first place. It argues forcefully to a generation that expects equality that without the right to decide whether to continue a pregnancy, a woman's autonomy and equality are compromised. It documents the critical role that access to abortion has played in women's lives over the past 30 years. Rather than focusing on whether we are about to lose *Roe* altogether, it exposes, defends against and attempts to

An Embryo Is Not a Person

A major effort at redefining the word "person" is taking place today. ... Biological and other scientific factors are being bent to accommodate the religious argument that a human being exists at conception, or when sperm meets egg.

The conceptus—weighing a very small fraction of an ounce—obviously is not an independent or autonomous human being, and certainly not a person, because it has no way to exist except in the body of another human being that feeds and protects it. ...

A human being and certainly a person is not determined solely by its biology at conception, when it has no sex, no brain, no eyes, ears or other senses. A "person" is determined only at birth, when it is welcomed into the human community as a living reality.

John M. Swomley, Human Quest, *January/February 2002.*

reverse the constant whittling away that diminishes the right to abortion every year. It focuses attention on the unfairness of laws that in effect deny this right to the most vulnerable women.

To defend abortion with confidence, we must first recognize that institutional opposition to the right is part of a broader campaign to undermine women's autonomy and equality. Antichoice leaders see sexuality (especially women's) divorced from procreation as shameful, women as inadequate to make weighty moral decisions and forced childbearing as appropriate punishment for sexual irresponsibility. They approve of requiring women to pay out of pocket for contraception, while ensuring that insurance plans cover men's access to

Viagra; reducing sexuality education to a "just say no" mantra and consigning those teenagers who say yes to the deadly risks of unprotected sex; and denying poor women the means to obtain abortions, yet refusing to help them provide adequate food, shelter and education for the children they bear. Abortion is only one piece of the puzzle.

When this puzzle is assembled, the image that emerges is of a woman subjugated, not a fetus saved. For example, it is illuminating that "right-to-life" leaders generally tolerate abortion in cases of rape or incest. The fetus conceived by rape is biologically and morally indistinguishable from the fetus conceived by voluntary intercourse. But in the view of our opponents, the rape victim is innocent while the woman who chooses to have sex is tainted. For them, it is the woman's innocence or guilt that determines whether she should be allowed to have an abortion or forced to bear a child.

The impulse to punish women rather than to help children is equally evident in the polities of antichoice states with regard to children already born. If the motivation behind abortion restrictions were really the love of babies, antichoice states should have child-friendly laws. Yet the opposite is so. A comprehensive review of the abortion and child welfare policies in the 50 states demonstrates that the states with the most restrictive abortion laws also spend the least to facilitate adoption, to provide subsistence to poor children and to educate children in general. The study concludes, "Pro-life states are less likely than pro-choice states to provide adequate care to poor and needy children. Their concern for the weak and vulnerable appears to stop at birth." The seemingly contradictory coexistence of "pro-life" laws and antichild polities is explained, in significant part, by opposition to women's changing roles in society: The more hostile statewide public opinion is toward women's equality and the lower women's income is relative to men's, the more likely the state is both to restrict abortion and to impoverish children.

In contrast, our position is prowoman, profamily, prochild and prochoice. This is a moral debate we must have and can win. Such a debate can move doubters to become moral defenders of a woman's decision to have an abortion. Even those who remain personally opposed to abortion may come to support each woman's right to make the decision in accordance with her own conscience, commitments and beliefs. What follows are some of the best reasons to support abortion rights.

Autonomy

A woman deciding whether to continue a pregnancy stands on moral ground. She is entitled to make her decision, and she must live with the consequences. No one else—and certainly not the government—should decide whether she will use her body to bring new life into the world. The decision is too intimate and too important to be taken from her.

In everyday life, men and women make decisions that affect the life and death of existing people. They decide whether to join the army; whether to donate blood, a kidney or bone marrow to a child; whether to give money to Save the Children instead of buying a new sweater, whether to decline a lifesaving blood transfusion; whether to drive a small fort on wheels that may protect its passengers in a crash but often kills those in less-substantial vehicles. Few question adults' autonomy to make these decisions, although some may criticize the individual choice made.

Yet, our opponents want a different standard to govern women's decisions about abortion. They portray women who demand the right to make this decision as selfish and immoral, although even many "prolifers" place fetuses on a lower moral plane than existing people (hence their tolerance of abortion in cases of rape and incest, among other inconsistencies). In response, we must staunchly defend women's ability and right to be moral actors, especially when they are making decisions about reproduction.

Equality

Without the right of reproductive choice, women cannot participate equally in the nation's social, political and economic life. Their freedom to decide whether and when to have children opens doors that would otherwise be closed. They may learn to be electricians, librarians, roofers, teachers or triathletes; care for their young children or aging parents; start and finish college; wait until they are financially and emotionally prepared to support a child; keep a steady job; marry if and when they want to.

Women still do the bulk of the work of raising children and caring for extended families. Whether they experience this work as a privilege, a necessity, a burden or all three, increasing their control over the scope and timing of these responsibilities can only help them to secure a more equal footing on whatever paths they travel. In fact, in countries throughout the world, women's desire and ability to limit the number of children they have go hand in hand with their educational advancement and economic independence.

Body Integrity

Women should have control over their own bodies. In virtually all other contexts, the law treats a person's body as inviolable. Prisoners are denied many of their most important personal liberties, yet are protected from unreasonable invasions of their bodies (such as routine body cavity searches). Similarly, the state cannot require a crime victim to undergo an operation to recover evidence (such as a bullet), even if that evidence would help to convict a murder suspect. And no law can force an unwilling parent to undergo bodily invasions far less risky than pregnancy (such as donating bone marrow) to save a living child. "It is difficult to imagine a clearer case of bodily intrusion" than for the government to demand that a woman continue a pregnancy and go through childbirth against her will.

Wantedness and Welcome

The decision to have a child—even more than the decision to have an abortion—carries profound moral implications. Unless a woman is willing to bear a child and give it up for adoption, she should have children when she feels she can welcome them. A mother's freedom to decide whether and when to have an additional child contributes immeasurably to the welfare of the children she already has, as well as any yet to be born. A teenager's decision to delay having a child until a time when she can provide adequate financial and emotional support increases the probability that when she does decide to have a family, it will be healthy and stable. Indeed, many women who decide not to have a child at a particular time do so out of reverence for children.

Personal and Public Health

Finally, the right to abortion promotes personal and public health. We know that criminal bans do not stop women from seeking abortions. The desperate measures women in pre-*Roe* days felt driven to take to terminate their unwanted pregnancies are testament to how untenable the prospect of childbearing can be. Access to safe, legal abortion ensures that women will not be maimed or killed when they decide they cannot continue a pregnancy. Similarly, access to safe abortion ensures that women can terminate pregnancies that endanger their health. A pregnant woman with a heart condition, uncontrolled hypertension, diabetes or one of a host of other problems must have all medically accepted options open to her. She, her loved ones and her doctor must be able to respond to shifting and serious health risks without having to consult a lawyer.

These reasons to support abortion rights are not new. All of them predate *Roe v. Wade,* some by centuries. Yet, as *Roe* turns 30 and continues its embattled advance toward middle age, these reasons are as pressing as ever. We state them in different ways to appeal to different audiences at different times, but all provide a basis for persuading people to stand behind abortion rights, both for themselves and for others.

> *"The number of unborn American children killed in the past 31 years is much higher than the total number of Americans killed in the entire history of our nation's wars."*

Abortion Is Not Ethical

Sam Brownback

In the following viewpoint Sam Brownback, a U.S. senator from Kansas, argues that abortion is unethical because it violates America's founding principles, which recognize and protect human rights. He maintains that scientific evidence clearly reveals the embryo to be a human life. As such, according to Brownback, the embryo has the same rights as any adult person, and killing it constitutes murder.

As you read, consider the following questions:

1. According to the author at what point in a fetus's development does medical science identify the unborn child as a human life?

2. What did Mother Teresa of Calcutta identify as the

Sam Brownback, "Abortion and the Conscience of the Nation Revisited," *Human Life Review*, Summer 2004. Copyright Human Life Foundation, Incorporated 2004. Reproduced by permission.

greatest destroyer of peace in the world today?

3. According to expert testimony in the Nebraska partial-birth abortion trial, at what stage of development does a fetus feel pain?

On Saturday, June 5, 2004, President Ronald Reagan was called into eternity. The depth of America's emotional outpouring in tribute to him was testimony to his character, and to the esteem in which his countrymen held him. Sadness naturally accompanies the passing of a loved one, but the time for weeping passes. We will always miss the Gipper, but we needn't look far to see the impact he left on this country. Reagan may have taken leave of this life, but he has left us his legacy.

That legacy was one of bold achievement in domestic, foreign, and social policy. Its unifying theme was a tremendous respect for each and every human life—wherever it lived, at whatever stage of development it had reached. This sensibility prompted Reagan to insist that the Soviet Empire was evil, and to demand of a new Soviet leader that he "tear down this wall"; it also led him to proclaim that "until and unless someone can establish that the unborn child is not a living human being, then that child is already protected by the Constitution, which guarantees life, liberty and the pursuit of happiness to all of us."

On January 14, 1988, Reagan made a simple yet profound presidential declaration of "the unalienable personhood of every American, from the moment of conception until natural death." Reagan articulated this principle—the Reagan Cultural Doctrine—throughout his years in the White House. He did so most notably in the spring of 1983 when—in a rare gesture for a sitting U.S. president—he submitted a soul-stirring policy essay to an intellectual journal. The article was "Abortion and the Conscience of the Nation," and it appeared in the *Human Life Review*.

The essay was typical of Reagan: clear, cogent, and filled with plain common sense. Essentially, Reagan argued that abortion violates human rights, and that it has a harmful effect on all people, not just its immediate victims. He noted that medical science, Western ethics, history, and the opinion of the American public are all on the side of life—as witnessed by their opposition to infanticide, which is closely linked with abortion. He appealed to Americans' support of human rights for all, whether born healthy or handicapped. He urged us to be souls of prayer, to work for positive change in society, and never to lose heart.

Assessing Progress Toward a Culture of Life

Twenty-one years later, and 31 years after *Roe v. Wade* [which legalized abortion], we need to revisit "Abortion and the Conscience of the Nation." We need to reflect on whether we are closer to—or further away from—having a culture of life. Perhaps most important, we need to contemplate what personal and legislative steps we must take to draw out the best in the freedom-loving, life-loving American spirit.

America retains her greatness and her goodness because a tremendous respect for every life continues to undergird our guiding principles. Reagan appealed to this respect for life—this culture of life—and the highest ideals in us all. It is to these ideals that we must urgently appeal today. Certainly, our culture may appear a little shaky right now—from same-sex unions in Massachusetts and San Francisco, to a comeback of eugenics, to abortion providers who give no thought to the pain of an unborn child. In fact, however, we are better than this. America's culture is better than this.

We have previously waged great cultural battles in America, and in these battles Divine Providence has led the way to tremendous victories, such as the abolition of slavery and deliverance from tyranny. True, victory is not for the fainthearted—but America has proven herself, time and again, the home of the brave.

Comparing Slavery and Abortion

Reagan appropriately alluded to the struggle against slavery in his essay. He compared the fight for the civil rights of African Americans with the fight for the rights of the unborn. This analogy is just as relevant today. Reagan wrote: "This is not the first time our country has been divided by a Supreme Court decision that denied the value of certain human lives. The Dred Scott decision of 1857 was not overturned in a day, or a year, or even a decade. At first, only a minority of Americans recognized and deplored the moral crisis brought about by denying the full humanity of our black brothers and sisters; but that minority persisted in their vision and finally prevailed. They did it by appealing to the hearts and minds of their countrymen, to the truth of human dignity under God."

As Reagan so eloquently noted, the Supreme Court is hardly infallible. Because of the sweeping *Roe v. Wade* and *Doe v. Bolton* Supreme Court decisions in 1973, abortion is available for all nine months of pregnancy, for any reason or for no reason at all. In *Roe* and *Doe*, seven justices unjustly dictated that the killing of the unborn is legal. This judicial activism was certainly not the voice of America but those two decisions nonetheless inaugurated an open season on the unborn; as a consequence, around 40 million babies have been killed in the womb since 1973. This statistic is all the more astonishing when you consider that the number of unborn American children killed in the past 31 years is much higher than the total number of Americans killed in the entire history of our nation's wars.

Embracing Higher Ideals

But bright days are ahead for our country, if we will only embrace its higher ideals. We caught a brief glimpse of what this looks like in the aftermath of [the September 11, 2001, terrorist attacks]. While mourning the loss of those murdered in the heinous terrorist attacks, Americans paused to reflect on the most important things—giving thanks for their lives and the lives of their loved ones. Our foremost principle, enshrined in our Declaration of Independence, remains as true as ever: "We hold these Truths to be self-evident, that all Men are created equal, that they are endowed by their Creator with certain unalienable Rights, that among these are Life . . . ." Life is beautiful, and Americans do cherish it. After 9/11, churches and memorial services were packed, as Americans recognized the continuing operation of Divine Providence within our vast world and universe.

Americans' spiritual reaction to 9/11 also manifested itself in selfless behavior. In the first few difficult days after the attacks, our nation's transportation infrastructure ground to a standstill; I heard many stories about perfect strangers driving to airports to take stranded travelers into their own homes. People turned off their televisions and spent a little more time with their families. The culture of death and its lies were spurned, because our conscience had been pricked.

This is profound evidence that the "shining city on a hill" still stands, even amidst the lashing storm of a culture of death. The shining city still has a conscience, and to this conscience we must appeal, on behalf of those who have no voice: the unborn. It is this kind of appeal that succeeded in delivering rights and freedom to African Americans; it will succeed again, in establishing protection for the unborn in their right to life, liberty, and the pursuit of happiness.

Scientific Evidence

We are armed in this appeal with the best evidence that medical science has to offer. Science is about the pursuit of truth in the service of mankind, and science tells us that the unborn child, from the moment of conception, is a human life. When those of us in the pro-life movement say that human life begins at conception, we are speaking about biology—not ideology, not belief, not ethics. Part of the difficulty in the current debate is caused by the (sometimes willful) confusion between science and ethics. Some engage in demagoguery against those who believe that all human life deserves protection, labeling them religious zealots who are trumpeting purely personal beliefs and seeking to impose those beliefs on others.

Ironically, though, it is these self-proclaimed defenders of science who are guilty of trampling on scientific truth. Nowhere is this more evident than in the debate over embryonic stem-cell research. A human embryo, unborn child, or human fetus is, biologically speaking, a young human life. To assert that it is not a life, or that it is merely a "potential life," is not a scientific statement. To assert that a human embryo is not a human life is to make an assertion of a personal belief completely unsupported by the facts of science; it is comparable to asserting that the sun revolves around the earth. Science unambiguously declares that the young human embryo is a human life.

Unfortunately, not everyone in this debate is looking at biology. But once both sides acknowledge the scientific truth—that the young human embryo or unborn child is a human life—then we can start to address what Reagan posited as the real question: "What is the value of a human life?" This is where the issue moves from biology, pure and simple, to ethics.

The Ethical Answer

And for Reagan—as for all those in the pro-life movement—the ethical answer is just as clear as the scientific one: The value of a human life is truly priceless. America was built upon the founding principle that every human being is endowed by its Creator with an inalienable right to life. And this founding principle was far from arbitrary. For the Founders, the inalienable right to life, granted by Divine

Diary of an Unborn Baby

- **Day 1** —fertilization: all human chromosomes are present; unique human life begins
- **Day 6** —embryo begins implanting in the uterus
- **Day 22** —heart begins to beat with the child's own blood, often a different type than the mother's
- **Week 5** —eyes, legs, hands begin to develop
- **Week 6** —brain waves detectable; mouth, lips present; fingernails forming
- **Week 7** —eyelids, toes form; nose distinct, baby kicking and swimming
- **Week 8** —every organ in place; bones begin to replace cartilage, fingerprints begin to form;
- **Weeks 9 and 10** —teeth begin to form, fingernails develop; baby can turn head, frown
- **Week 11** —baby can grasp objects placed in hand; all organ systems functioning; the baby has fingerprints, a skeletal structure, nerves, and circulation
- **Week 12** —the baby has all of the parts necessary to experience pain, including the nerves, spinal cord and thalamus; the baby is nearing the end of the first trimester

National Right to Life Committee. www.nrlc.org.

Providence, was the linchpin that held everything together. In a letter on slavery, written in 1782, Thomas Jefferson went so far as to ask: "Can the liberties of a nation be thought secure when we have removed their only firm basis, a conviction in the minds of the people that these liberties are the gift of God? That they are not to be violated but with his wrath? Indeed I tremble for my country when I reflect that God is just: that his justice cannot sleep forever."

Jefferson was writing about slaves. But his statement is equally applicable to unborn children, because they, too, are undeniably human. Every human life—from the moment of conception until natural death—is sacred because, as our Founders believed, every human being has been created in the image of a living and holy God. Human beings are an end unto themselves, not a means to an end—even a good end, such as the advance of scientific knowledge.

In a passionate plea at the National Prayer Breakfast in 1994, Blessed Mother Teresa of Calcutta said: "I feel that the greatest destroyer of peace today is abortion, because it is a war against the child, a direct killing of the innocent child, murder by the mother herself. And if we accept that a mother can kill even her own child, how can we tell other people not to kill one another?" On the value of human life, there was no greater authority in the 20th century than Mother Teresa. She was an incredibly beautiful woman; I have never met a person with a more beautiful soul. My meeting with her was brief, but I will be forever affected by her words and the love and fire that I saw in her eyes when I helped her into her car as she departed from the U.S. Capitol in the spring of 1997. This was a woman who loved everyone. Her authoritative words should be reflected upon by every abortion provider: "Please don't kill the child. I want the child. Please give me the child. I am willing to accept any child who would be aborted and to give that child to a married couple who will love the child and be loved by the child."

Mother Teresa may be gone, but her sisters continue to live that spirit of charity every single day. As a society, we must do the same: We must cherish every life. If we abandon respect for the life of the one-hour-old human embryo or the one-month-old fetus, we are truly on the slippery slope that leads to the abandonment of the positive law against murder—which is, after all, based on the premise that life is a gift of God. . . .

Valuing All Categories of Human Life

Embryo, fetus, infant, child, and adult are categories of human development; they are all human life. Whether one is physically healthy or ill, emotionally healthy or ill—these, too, are categories of human life, and thus do not make individuals less worthy of protection. As Reagan wrote: "We cannot diminish the value of one category of human life—the unborn—without diminishing the value of all human life." All human life—no matter how it is categorized, or what its "quality" may be—should be esteemed and valued.

There are, of course, some callous souls in our land. Consider, for example, the lack of reverence for life displayed by the mother who "selectively" aborted two of three healthy children so that she could continue to live the kind of a life she preferred. (Her story was told this past summer [2004] in a *New York Times* article headlined "When One Is Enough.") And consider the abortion providers who testified in the recent partial-birth-abortion-ban trial in New York. In one exchange, the judge asked the abortionist: "Do you tell [the mother] whether or not it will hurt the fetus?" The abortionist responded, "The intent [is] that the fetus will die during the process of uterine evacuation." The judge persisted, "Ma'am, I didn't ask you that . . . Do you tell them whether or not that hurts the fetus?" The abortionist flippantly replied: "I have never talked to a fetus about whether or not they experience pain." Another abortionist, when asked by the judge whether partial-birth abortion hurts the baby, responded, "I don't know." The judge pressed, "But you go ahead and do it anyway, is that right?" The abortion provider responded, "Yes, I go ahead and do it." . . .

There are brighter days ahead because the public is moving to the side of life, and our national conscience does remain sensitive. We are practical people, but we have a big heart and know right from wrong. We call our shots with our mind, informed by our heart.

Scientific advances have already contributed to this pro-life trend, by increasing our knowledge of life inside the womb. Today's 4-D Ultrasound technology leaves little doubt that a human being is alive and growing inside her mother's womb. Consider, too, the testimony of medical expert Dr. Kanwaljeet Sonny Anand in the Nebraska partial-birth-abortion trial. Dr. Anand testified that "the fetus is very likely extremely sensitive to pain during the gestation of 20 to 30 weeks. And so the procedures associated with the partial-birth abortion . . . would be likely to cause severe pain." . . .

Young People Are Increasingly Pro-Life

There is special cause for optimism in the fact that young people, more than any other demographic, are increasingly pro-life. Perhaps this is because many of their peers—more than 40 million of them—have been aborted. One of these aborted children could have grown up to be one of my own children's playmates; another could have become one of their future spouses. This is a tragedy, and our young people know it.

To be an American in the fullest sense is to be a life-loving, freedom-loving soul. Reagan concluded his *Human Life Review* essay with a great appeal for prayer and perseverance in the pro-life struggle that lay ahead. He wrote that "there is no cause more important for preserving that freedom than affirming the transcendent right to life of all human beings, the right without which no other rights have any meaning." Reagan knew that affirming the sanctity and dignity of every human life would not be an easy or painless task. Accordingly, he urged prayer, diligence, and trust in Divine Providence; and he appealed to the example of William Wilberforce, the great English statesman, whose lifelong crusade for the abolition of slavery in the British Empire was fulfilled on his deathbed. We need the same, if not more, intensity of prayer now.

Our Supreme Court's decision in *Roe* is certainly not the final word on the issue of abortion, just as the Court was not the final word on slavery in Dred Scott. Our system gives us the opportunity to rectify past wrongs. It is my fervent hope and prayer for America that we base our laws on what science tells us: namely, that the young human embryo is a human life. I believe that I will live to see the end of the abortion industry, and the sanctity and dignity of every human life affirmed. Until then, abortion will continue to prod the conscience of our nation. Great labors remain before us, but the rights and lives of unborn children are absolutely worth our efforts.

Reagan was our first great pro-life president, and surely others will follow in his footsteps. His legacy endures and the pro-life movement continues to make steady progress. We have come a long way since Reagan's 1983 essay, and we have a long way to go, but we are on the right track. On behalf of the unborn, let us pray and persevere; and may God bless America.

| "Women have a basic human right to
| decide what to do about a pregnancy."

Abortion Protects Women's Rights

Frances Kissling

In this viewpoint Frances Kissling argues that a woman has a right to decide whether or not to continue a pregnancy. This right is supported by other well-established human rights, such as the right to bodily integrity and the right to health, Kissling contends. She asserts that in a just society, a woman's right to abortion is protected. Kissling is president of Catholics for a Free Choice, an independent not-for-profit organization engaged in research, policy analysis, education, and advocacy on issues of gender equality and reproductive health.

As you read, consider the following questions:

1. What three central values does the author believe should be part of public conversation about abortion?
2. The author imagines a world in which a fetus could be removed from the womb to develop in an alternate

environment. In the author's experience, why have some women opposed the idea of such continued existence for the fetus?

3. What are some examples of scientific advances that affect the way people think about a fetus, according to Kissling?

I believe women have a basic human right to decide what to do about a pregnancy. Other well-established human rights concepts bolster this argument including bodily integrity, the right to health, the right to practice one's religion (or not) and the right to be free from religious laws in modern democratic societies. Despite the assertions of some very intelligent prolifers that the abortion issue is a question of the human rights of the fetus, the human rights community is moving steadily towards recognizing a woman's right to choose and there is no countervailing view in this community that even considers the question of whether or not fetuses are rights-bearing entities.

But the abortion issue is not one in which only rights are at stake. There are at least three central values that need to be part of the public conversation about abortion and, as appropriate, influence behavior, if not law. They are:

1. The human right of women to decide whether or not to continue a pregnancy.

2. A respect for human life that takes the form of what Daniel Callahan [cofounder of The Hastings Center, a bioethics research organization] called more than 30 years ago a moral presumption in favor of life.

3. A commitment to ensure that provisions which permit the taking of life (whether it be fetal, animal or plant) not coarsen the overall fabric of society and our attitudes toward each other as well as toward developing human life.

Women's Right to Decide

First, and I would say primary, is our obligation to respect in law and social thought the right of women to bodily autonomy. Generally speaking, nobody should be forced to carry a pregnancy to term without their consent. I am revolted by the thought that a law banning most or all abortions would, if it were to be more than a rhetorical exercise, require an enforcement mechanism that actively forces women to continue pregnancies that they believe to be antithetical to their needs or identities. But the right to choose abortion is not absolute, and in practice and law even those of us most ardently prochoice do not demand absolutism. The law clearly does not recognize that the right is so fundamental that it requires the government to provide abortion services routinely for free. The first restriction of [*Roe v. Wade*, which legalized abortion] was the court decision that freed the federal government from the obligation to provide funding for abortions for women dependent on the government for their medical care. Medical ethics, on the other hand, demands that a patient who arrives at a health service at death's door must be treated even if he or she has no money. Our clinics turn away some women who cannot afford abortions. We insist on full payment in advance, sometimes delaying an abortion until the pregnancy is further advanced and carries a greater risk of complications.

Many accept that post-viability [the point at which a fetus can survive outside the womb] abortions can be denied unless the woman's life is at risk, the fetus has a condition that is truly incompatible with life or there is a serious health risk to the woman. We are thus prepared to "force," or at least not to facilitate an abortion at eight months for a woman who is, for example, abandoned by her partner and no longer wishes to have a child. But, with those limits acknowledged, we believe a good society will make it possible for women who do not want to be pregnant to get safe, dignified and compassionate abortion services. It will also do everything it can to help women and men prevent pregnancies if they do not want to have children. This is not necessarily out of respect for the fetus, but out of respect for women. The act of taking life in abortion is defensible and can have positive results, but in and of itself is not a moral good. We should do everything we can to enable people to live lives that affirm human beings and other forms of life that are not harmful to our world. One colleague who reviewed this article noted that the term "right to life" and its unrelenting and vague formulation obscures the fact that some life is dangerous and does not deserve to be respected. Cancer cells are a form of life as are viruses like polio and HIV/AIDS. Should they be respected?

Valuing Fetal Life

This brings us to the second value of a good society: respect for life, including fetal life. Why should we allow this value to be owned by those opposed to abortion? Are we not capable of walking and chewing gum at the same time; of valuing life and respecting women's rights? Have we not ceded too much territory to antiabortionists by not articulating the value of fetal life? . . .

Such an effort will take a lot of work and involve exposing deep differences among supporters of choice regarding our views on the inherent value of fetal life on its own terms and in relation to women's rights. An interesting thought exercise might help to clarify what prochoice (and anti–abortion) leaders believe about fetal value. Imagine a world in which it was possible to remove fetuses prior to viability from women's bodies and allow them to develop in a nonuterine environment. Perhaps they could be implanted in men or other women who want them; perhaps they could develop in a specially equipped nursery? In this world, medicine is so far advanced that this could be accomplished painlessly and without risking the health of either the woman or the fetus. Of course, this is at present largely a fantasy and by that time we would have found the ideal, risk-free, failure-free contraceptive; but let's pretend.

What are the first five concerns and reactions that come to your mind? Is one of them the fact that this would mean fetuses need not die? My own experience in presenting this option to both advocates and opponents of abortion is that the fetus's life is rarely a consideration. Among the most interesting reactions of those who are prochoice is a concern that some women might find the continued existence of the fetus painful for them or that women have a right to ensure that their genetic material does not enter the world. Abortion in this sense becomes the guarantee of a dead fetus, if desired, rather than the removal of the fetus from an unwilling host, the woman. To even offer women such an option is, some think, cruel. For some the right to choose abortion seems to include the right to be protected from thinking about the fetus and from any pain that might result from others talking about the fetus in value-laden terms. In this construct, it is hard to identify any value fetal life might have.

This level of sensitivity to protecting women from their feelings takes other forms. For example, some prochoice advocates have objected to public discussion of abortion that includes concern for the number of abortions that occur in the US or has as its goal reducing the number of abortions. Some bristled at President Clinton's formula that abortion should be "safe, legal and rare." If abortion is justifiable why should it be rare? Even the suggestion that abortion is a moral matter as well as a legal one has caused concern that such a statement might make women feel guilty. Words like "baby" are avoided, not just because they are inaccurate, but because they are loaded.

Chris Britt. Reproduced by permission.

In a society where women have long been victims of moral discourse, these concerns are somewhat understandable, but they do not contribute much towards convincing people that when prochoice people say they value fetal life it is more than lip service.

The reaction of antiabortionists to the idea that a fetus could be removed from the body of an unwilling woman is as troubling. Again, one rarely hears cries of joy that fetal lives would be saved. The focus also is on the woman. But here, the view that women are, by their nature, made for childbearing dominates. Women have an obligation to continue pregnancies, to suffer the consequences of their sexuality. It is unnatural to even think that fetuses could become healthy and happy people if they did not spend nine months in the womb of a woman. One is led to believe that, for those opposed to abortion, it is not saving fetuses that matters but preserving a social construct in which women breed. . . .

When the Fetus Becomes a Person

Once one moves away from the narrow question of when the fetus becomes a person to the more meaningful question of what value does the fetus have and when that value emerges, it becomes difficult to develop an ethical formula for assigning value and asserting the obligations that flow from that value. There is a wide range of respectable opinion on these questions and few hard and fast conclusions.

But the need to offer some answers from a prochoice perspective is both morally and politically urgent. Those opposed to abortion have moved aggressively for laws that depend on the recognition of the fetus as a person, as a rights-bearing entity. At the same time, there are scientific advances that affect the way we think about the fetus and indeed make it more present among us. For some, these realities lead to a greater connection to fetal life; perhaps not as a person, but as part of the continuum of what we are, of humanity. Examples include 3-D and 4-D pictures of fetuses in utero that appear to be awake, asleep, walking, yawning—engaging in activities that are related to human identity—and the few, very few, very premature babies who struggle and appear to have a great determination to live. Even the reality that pre-embryos used to create stem cells that may ultimately save the lives of thousands makes the embryo more human and more valuable—it can give as well as receive, even at a stage of development that bears little resemblance to even fetal life. Of course, there is an element of my ode to the embryo that is poetic and romantic, even anthropomorphic, as the embryo does not consciously "give;" it is instead useful, but nonetheless that usefulness is a positive quality that should not be feared, but appreciated.

The fetus is indeed a wondrous part of our humanity; we are drawn to it as part of the ongoing mystery of who we are. Do we not question our own value and why we are here, what we contribute and what we take from the world? There is of course a danger in over-romanticizing fetal life or in defining its value primarily in relation to ourselves. For an infertile couple who deeply want a child, someone else's fetus is very precious and potentially their child. For a woman who has been raped, that fetus may well be seen as a monster. The relation of value to wantedness complex and at times troubling. Antiabortionists have countered the "Every child a wanted child" message by pointing out that if wantedness is what gives us value and a right to life, then who among the unwanted will be the next to be declared disposable—the sick, the disabled, the poor or the unemployed? . . .

Coarsening Attitudes Toward Fetal Life

For me, a more troubling question is whether or not regular exposure to the taking of life in abortion or the defense of a right to choose abortion would, if not addressed, lead to a coarsening of attitude toward fetal life. The inability of prochoice leaders to give any specific examples of ways in which respect for fetal life can be demonstrated or to express any doubt about any aspect of abortion suggests that such a hardening of the heart is possible. This concern or possibility does not lead me to say that abortion should become illegal, more restricted, more stigmatized. It does lead me to believe that we would do well as prochoice people to present abortion as a complex issue that involves loss—and to be saddened by that loss at the same time as we affirm and support women's decisions to end pregnancies. Is there not a way to simply say, "Yes, it is sad, unfortunate, tragic (or whatever word you are comfortable with) that this life could not come to fruition. It is sad that we live in a world where there is so little social and economic support for families that many women have no choice but to end pregnancies. It is sad that so many women do not have access to contraception. It is sad that this fetus was not healthy enough to survive and it was good that this

Unintended Pregnancy Is a Continuing Reality

Regardless of the legal status of abortion, its fundamental underlying cause—unintended pregnancy—has been a continuing reality for American women. In the 1960s, researchers from Princeton University estimated that almost one in three Americans (32%) who wanted no more children were likely to have at least one unintended pregnancy before the end of their child bearing years; more than six in 10 Americans (62%) wanting children at some point in the future were likely to have experienced at least one unintended pregnancy.

While the problem of unintended pregnancy spanned all strata of society, the choices available to women varied before [*Roe v. Wade* legalized abortion]. At best, these choices could be demeaning and humiliating, and at worst, they could lead to injury and death. Women with financial means had some, albeit very limited, recourse to a legal abortion; less affluent women, who disproportionately were young and members of minority groups, had few options aside from a dangerous illegal procedure.

The Alan Guttmacher Institute, March 2003.

woman had the right to make this choice for herself and her family, to avoid suffering, and to act on her values and her sense of what her life should be."

Are there not ways to affirm and protect the right to choose abortion while actively promoting policies which would actually enhance reflection and good decision making and supporting voluntary mechanisms for nonjudgmental reflection and alternatives to abortion? For example, should we not combine our support for the right of adolescent girls to decide to have an abortion with greater efforts to involve their parents, including seeking funding for counseling for teens facing the abortion decision and their parents as an alternative to mandatory parental consent and notification laws? Surely we agree that young women aged 13, 14, 15 (and even older) need their parents at this time? And surely, our response to date which implies that only teens who are at risk from their parents choose not to tell them rings hollow in the ears of most parents who know that their kids are loath to tell them where they are going on Saturday afternoon, let alone that they are pregnant? The youngest of teens should not have to face an abortion or any medical procedure alone. This is not just about rights; it is a matter of health, safety and compassion. . . .

It has long been a truism of the abortion debate that those who are prochoice have rights and those who are against legal abortion have morality; that those who support abortion rights concentrate on women and those opposed focus on the fetus. After 30 years of legal abortion and a debate that shows no signs of ending and has no clear winner—is it not time to try and combine rights and morality, to consider both women and developing human life? Ultimately, abortion is not a political question and politics will not end the enormous conflict over abortion. Abortion is a profoundly moral question and any movement that fails to grapple with and respect all the values at stake in crafting a social policy about abortion will be inadequate in its effort to win the support of the majority of Americans.

| "Created life must always and under all circumstances have the right to be born."

Abortion Violates the Rights of the Unborn

Charles I. Lugosi

A central issue in the abortion debate concerns when the fetus acquires rights as an individual human being. In the following viewpoint Charles I. Lugosi asserts that the unborn fetus is a human being with human and constitutional rights from the time of conception. Therefore, he contends that abortion is morally wrong. Lugosi teaches constitutional law and bioethics at St. Thomas University.

As you read, consider the following questions:

1. In the case of *People v. Kurr*, the Court of Appeals held that nonviable fetuses are entitled to protection from unlawful assault. What did this court say about the rights of the fetus in a medical abortion?

Dr. Charles I. Lugosi, S.J.D., M.B.E., LL.M., LL.B, "Respecting Human Life in 21st Century America: A Moral Perspective to Extend Civil Rights to the Unborn from Creation to Natural Death," *Issues in Law and Medicine*, vol. 20, 2005, pp. 254–258. Reprinted with permission of the St. Louis University Law Journal. © St. Louis University School of Law, St. Louis, Missouri.

2. Who does the author suggest might be appointed to advocate for the civil liberties of the unborn?

3. According to the author, what is the most practical and effective first step toward ensuring dignity and respect for all persons?

There is a moral imperative to affirm and constitutionally confer the status of personhood upon all living human organisms at the time of creation. This moral imperative represents our society's rejection of inequality and all forms of human slavery. Extending constitutional protection to all members of the human family is consistent with liberal equality. Civil libertarians must not hesitate when it comes to speaking out on the ethics of destroying and exploiting innocent unborn human beings. Not to do so, is sheer hypocrisy.

Pro-abortion feminists resent discrimination against all women on the basis of sex, yet they engage in wholesale discrimination against unborn human beings, including females, on the basis of age, size and power. These same feminists reject the notion that marriage results in ownership by their husband, but insist that they own their unborn children and may harm or kill them at their whim. Feminists love their freedom and hate having their fate decided by the choice of any other person, especially a man. Yet, these same women insist the decision whether or not to abort their unborn children is a matter of choice belonging exclusively to the mother and no one else.

Women, who do not understand that an abortion terminates the life of a human being, cannot exercise choice responsibly and cannot give legally valid informed consent to an abortion. On October 29, 2002, in *Acuna v. Turkish*, the Appellate Division of the Superior Court of New Jersey allowed a common law tort claim for emotional distress by a twenty-nine-year-old mother of two children who gave her doctor consent to abort her eight-week-old fetus. When the pregnant woman asked her doctor "if there was a baby already in [her,]" she received the answer, "don't be stupid, it's only blood." At trial, the doctor testified, "a seven-week pregnancy is not a human being." Rose Acuna's lawsuit against Dr. Sheldon Turkish was eventually dismissed by Superior Court Judge Amy Chambers, who ruled in November 2003 that informed consent did not extend to answering a patient's question about whether she was about to terminate the life of a living human being.

A Woman's Right to Protect Her Unborn Children

Does a pregnant woman who knows she is carrying unborn children have the legal right to kill someone who is attempting to harm her fetuses? In *People v. Kurr*, Jaclyn Kurr was seventeen weeks pregnant with quadruplets when she stabbed and killed her abusive boyfriend who unlawfully punched her twice in the stomach during an argument regarding his cocaine use. She suffered a miscarriage a few weeks later. In Michigan, a person may kill someone in lawful defense of another. At trial, the judge withheld from the jury Kurr's defense of protecting "another," on the basis that her fetuses were not viable and therefore not human beings. She was convicted of voluntary manslaughter.

On October 4, 2002, the Court of Appeals ordered a new trial, because Kurr was wrongfully denied the defense of protecting another, and was thereby deprived of her constitutional right to due process. The court held that non-viable fetuses are entitled to protection from unlawful assault, although not from a lawful assault as permitted by [*Roe v. Wade*, which legalized abortion] during a medical abortion.

Permitting Kurr this defense is consistent with the public policy behind Michigan's fetal protection statute. The case has been appealed to the Michigan Supreme Court, which may hear arguments as to when human life begins.[1]

Biology Tells When a Human Is Created

In the final analysis, all of us are compelled to return to biology to answer the question of when a human being is created. To not answer this question is itself an answer and places the power of life and death with those people who hold values inconsistent with equality and respect for the sanctity of all living human organisms. This is an invitation to social, political, and cultural disaster. Even the death of one unborn child makes a difference.

The United States Supreme Court will hopefully not squander another opportunity to stop the deaths of millions of unborn children and will declare that constitutional personhood begins from the time of conception. The Court may benefit from the appointment of legal guardians to advocate for the civil liberties of the unborn. The continued denial of legal personhood to the unborn is a means to achieve various utilitarian ends and invites judges to turn a blind eye to reality. Personhood is an imaginary status that cannot alter the biological fact of humanity. [Jed Rubenfield argues that]

> And personhood is not a matter of fact. It is not a thing or a concrete property inhering in a thing. It is a status, legal and moral, that we confer as a normative matter at a certain point in human development. Stripped of any reifying (or theifying) premises, personhood is no different in its conceptual structure from another status conferred later in life: adulthood.

Philosophy that is disconnected from biological truth is of little worth in the debate regarding the value of incipient human life. The legal and moral distinction between person and

1. On January 22, 2003, the Michigan Supreme Court denied appeal.

Are There Cases in Which Abortion Is the Best Option?

Following are three case histories in which an unexpected pregnancy has complicated life for the parents as well as the potential future life of the unborn child. Based on each situation, would you advise abortion?

1. [There is] a preacher and wife who are living in dire poverty. They already have 14 children. Now the wife [discovers she is] pregnant [again]. Considering their strained [financial] circumstances and the excessive world population, would you [recommend] an abortion?

2. A [man] is sick with syphilis. [His wife] has [tuberculosis]. They have four children. The first is blind, the second was stillborn, the third is deaf, and the fourth has TB. [Now their mother is] pregnant again. Given the high probability that the baby will be born congenitally handicapped, would you recommend abortion?

3. A teenage girl, 14–15 years old, is pregnant. [She is] not married. Her fiancé is not the father of the baby, and [he is] very upset. Would you [recommend] an abortion?

How did you answer? In the first case, if you said yes, you have just killed John Wesley, a great evangelist of the 18th century and founder of Methodism. In the second case, you would have killed Ludwig van Beethoven. If you said yes in the third case, you [would have] consented to the [death] of Jesus Christ.

Francis Marsden, Credo for Catholic Times,
November 21, 2000.

human being must be harmonized if there is to be true equality and fairness among all members of the human family. Justice requires that there be laws to uphold the sanctity of all human life, from the very beginning to the very end of life.

Lessons Learned

Wisdom comes at the price of suffering. It is very helpful to listen to what German scientists, sensitive to the evil potential of human medical experimentation, now say after the lessons of the Nazi regime:

> The determination of the beginning of human life by another human being cannot be objective as this determination is a function of an individual value system and what that individual believes to be essential. The description of the human embryo in terms of a successively differentiating cell mass does not mean that this model can be used in the same way for questions involving moral judgment. Ethical statements always include the point of view and the value system of the person making the statement. To answer the question about the beginning of personal dignity does not mean describing a natural phenomenon but deciding on value in moral and ethical terms. Biological realities do not include moral standards. The status of an embryo is a dignity, which is bestowed on it. It is not based on its own inner quality but on an attitude towards the embryo from autonomous subjects. . . .
>
> In Germany, the general opinion is, however, that despite the existence of different values and interests, unborn human life has an inalienable right to human dignity and protection. Because this dignity is not a fact which can be determined empirically, it is not bound to certain abilities or value judgments. Human dignity cannot be divided and is of value in principle from the very beginning [from H.W. Michelmann & B. Hinney, *Science & Engineering Ethics*, 1995].

If bioethicists like [Peter] Singer are successful in persuading Americans to maintain and expand the membership of Depersonalized Humans to attain utilitarian objectives, the cost will be the abandonment of those civil libertarian values upon which this nation was founded. It is not a matter of getting rid of values in a secular society; the war is between utilitarian philosophy and traditional ideas of liberal equality.

Honoring the Sanctity of Human Life

There is a moral imperative for all true civil libertarians to reject all attempts to classify human beings according to personhood criteria. "Quality of life" is no substitute for the "sanctity of human life." Sanctity of life offers the best approach to protect our civil liberties and to ensure dignity and respect for all persons—as this article defines persons. The most practical and effective first step to reach this goal is to vigorously defend the right to life of the unborn human.

The assessment of the right of a human embryo for protection according to utilitarian, genetic, morphological, or race-ideological points of view result in grading and limiting life protection. The protection of the individual human being has to be valid uniformly during its stages in the same manner and from the very beginning. It must not depend on phases of development, so-called "degrees of humanity," because then they would be criteria of selection. Created life must always and under all circumstances have the right to be born.

The abortion issue is at the core of the moral debate over exploitation and oppression of Depersonalized Humans. That is where the decisive battle against human slavery in the Twenty-first Century will continue to be fought and ultimately won. Either the unborn are human beings and are constitutional persons or they are not. How this question is ultimately answered will determine how our society will be judged by future generations.

Human from Conception

The unborn are human beings and persons from the time of conception. The legal distinction between a person and human being must be abolished if we are to live in a society of equals. In a free and democratic society like America, there is no place for a class of Depersonalized Humans. Constitutional personhood and protection of all human beings must begin from the time of their creation and continue until natural death.

It remains to be seen whether civil libertarians will continue to abdicate their role as the guardian of all the oppressed and accept the challenge to abolish the laws that have revived a new form of human slavery in Twenty-first Century America.

> *"There are no studies that show [partial-birth abortion] is a more dangerous procedure or that it leads to problems getting pregnant in the future."*

Partial Birth Abortions Do Not Harm Women

Rob Deters

In the viewpoint that follows, University of Wisconsin law student Rob Deters argues that partial birth abortion procedures are safe and ethical. He explains that partial birth abortion, more accurately called intact dilation and extraction, is a procedure in which a nonviable fetus is removed from a woman's uterus sixteen or more weeks into the pregnancy. Deters claims that no studies show that dilation and extraction is dangerous, and he contends that the procedure has medical benefits. In November 2003, shortly after he wrote this viewpoint, the Partial Birth Abortion Ban Act was passed. It prohibits abortions in which a living fetus is intentionally killed while partly or completely outside the mother's body.

As you read, consider the following questions:

1. According to Deters, why do dilation and extraction procedures exist?
2. What is the argument over dilation and extraction all about, in the author's contention?
3. How many dilation and extraction procedures were performed in 1996, according to Deters?

L et's be clear. Abortion is not murder. If it were, the Supreme Court would not uphold it as constitutional. If it were, the American Medical Association, whose opinion on health and ethics I hold in high esteem, wouldn't support abortion as a viable medical procedure. Abortion is murder only if you choose to define it as such, but there is no such definition that you can make every rational person believe.

"Partial-Birth Abortions" Are Necessary

Partial-birth abortion, or, more accurately, intact dilation and extraction, is a technique by which a non-viable fetus is removed from a woman's uterus. The skull of the fetus is collapsed via a cervical incision and suction rather than crushed with forceps.

The other technique used at this stage in a woman's pregnancy is dilation and evacuation, which calls for the dismemberment of the body of the fetus with forceps and its removal from the uterus.

No law to ban "partial-birth abortions" prohibits this second procedure, just the first.

All abortions are performed with the end result being the destruction of a fetus; it's simply the method that we're discussing. You can scrape, suck, crush or surgically remove fetal tissue from a woman all for the same purpose—to terminate a pregnancy.

Why does this technique even exist? Dilation and extraction is simply an option for a doctor to use when a woman is at a very specific point in her pregnancy. At 16 weeks into a pregnancy, a fetal skull is too large to pass through a non-dilated cervix. At 17 weeks, the bones in a fetus begin to calcify, leading to a higher probability of injury to a woman's uterus because of bony fragments.

These two techniques are options for a doctor to choose from in order to perform the abortion in the safest way possible. At 24 weeks (the end of the second trimester) abortions are outlawed as a voluntary procedure and are only performed if there is a medical emergency.

The Politics of Abortion

The argument over dilation and extraction is all about politics, not about a woman's health. There are no studies that show dilation and extraction is a more dangerous procedure or that it leads to problems getting pregnant in the future. In fact, many doctors feel the procedure has many benefits, including fewer instruments used in the uterus, less chance of infection and shorter operating time.

Squeamish yet? Of course you are. That's exactly how conservatives want you to feel. They want to use the natural reaction we have to this medical procedure (feeling uncomfortable) to make an argument that just doesn't hold. In fact, it doesn't hold in courts of law very much at all.

Previous attempts to limit dilation and extraction have all been struck down. [In 2000] the Supreme Court in *Stenberg vs. Carhart* ruled that Nebraska's ban on dilation and extraction was unconstitutional. It cited two reasons: there was no exception for the woman's health, and the ban placed an "undue burden" on the woman's right to choose. Although it was a close call (a 5–4 vote), it still didn't pass muster.

The current law being discussed in conference committee at the Capitol in Washington, D.C., is little different.

Many opponents of the "partial-birth abortion" ban that just passed both the House and the Senate (it's simply being revised) say it will take just a matter of time until the Supreme

Banning a Safe Procedure Threatens Women's Health

A threat to women's health *always* results when a safe medical procedure is removed from the physician's array of options, as there will always be some woman for whom the banned procedure would be the safest.

A wealth of medical evidence supports the conclusion that D&X [dilation and extraction] is a safe procedure that may well be the safest option for some women.

American Civil Liberties Union,
Letter to the Senate Urging Opposition to the
So-Called "Partial Birth Abortion Ban Act of 2003,"
October 1, 2003.

Court strikes it down just like it did Nebraska's law. This is probably true, but the narrow margin of the previous decision doesn't make this an absolute.[1]

Governmental Intrusion

What is really going on here is far more pernicious. "Partial-birth abortion" is a scare campaign. It's a way for conservatives to pounce on a tiny fact, blow it up out of proportion and make political hay.

If dilation and extraction is so terrible and we have to limit it by law, it must be rampant, right? Wrong. In 1996, the last year for which statistics are available, there were 1.4 million abortions performed in this country. Of them, only 650 were "partial-birth abortions."

1. In February 2006 the Supreme Court agreed to hear a case that challenged the constitutionality of the ban.

Conservatives believe that a government that governs the least governs the best. For conservatives, when it comes to morality, a government that is the most intrusive is the ideal.

Currently, many of this nation's conservatives are demanding abstinence-only sex education, taking stands against the decriminalization of drugs and legislating that marriage be defined by law as between a man and a woman. This is fundamentalism at its most obvious. Conservatives—Republicans or not—demand your lifestyle, your choices and your options be limited to those with which they themselves feel comfortable.

A woman's right to choose is based on a simple premise: A fetus is not a person until it can live outside the womb. Until that point, it is up to the woman, for health, personal, economic or social reasons, to either carry to term or terminate that pregnancy. There is no "child" and there is no "person"—there is a thing.

> "The [partial-birth abortion] ban has succeeded in educating society and in swaying public opinion to help the unborn."

A Partial-Birth Abortion Ban Would Protect Unborn Children

Antony Barone Kolenc

In this viewpoint Antony Barone Kolenc lists two reasons to support a ban on partial-birth abortion. First, he claims that the procedure constitutes infanticide (killing an infant) rather than abortion (expulsion of a fetus). Second, he states that the procedure causes pain to the unborn child. Antony Barone Kolenc teaches constitutional law at the U.S. Air Force Academy and supports pro-life, anti-abortion legislation. The Partial-Birth Abortion Ban Act of 2003 was struck down as unconstitutional not long after being signed into law. On July 15, 2005, the 8th U.S. Circuit Court of Appeals upheld the lower courts' decisions.

Antony Barone Kolenc, "Legal Failure or Moral Success," *America*, vol. 191, November 29, 2004, pp. 11–14. Copyright America Press, Inc., 2002. All rights reserved. Reproduced by permission of America Press. For subscription information, visit www .americamagazine.com.

As you read, consider the following questions:

1. By the end of the 1990s, how many states had passed legislation banning the partial-birth abortion procedure?

2. What key provision that had caused President Bill Clinton to veto previous partial-birth abortion bans did Congress intentionally leave out of the 2003 ban?

3. According to Supreme Court Justice Anthony Kennedy, what is the important difference between partial-birth abortion and other abortion methods?

Partial-birth abortion came to public attention in 1992 during a presentation given by Marvin Haskell, M.D., to the National Abortion Federation. Some doctors claim to have performed similar techniques since the 1970's. When the American public discovered the facts about partial-birth abortion, many united to speak on behalf of the unborn. A political movement took shape to ban the procedure. The issue became the new rallying cry for the pro-life movement

Overnight, the procedure was tagged as the most inhumane method of abortion, causing severe pain to an unborn child who is already in the process of a live birth. The method is commonly compared to infanticide, because the child is almost entirely delivered before the abortion doctor brutally ends his or her life. This is done by crushing the child's skull just moments before the first breath.

Religious leaders and politicians spoke out, putting the partial-birth abortion issue at center stage in America's abortion debate. The pursuit of a legal ban became a defining issue for the pro-life movement. For their part, pro-abortion groups opposed the ban as an attempt to overturn *Roe v. Wade*, the 1973 Supreme Court case that legalized abortion. As both sides marched into battle, the pursuit of a successful ban catapulted the issue onto an emotional and legal roller coaster ride.

By the end of the 1990's, many Christians and other pro-life activists rejoiced that 30 states had banned the cruel procedure, but their victory celebration was short-lived. In *Stenberg v. Carhart*, a Supreme Court decision in 2000, a sharply divided court struck down Nebraska's partial-birth abortion ban as a violation of the U.S. Constitution. The court decided that the ban was too broad and might place an "undue burden" on a woman's ability to choose other "legal" methods of abortion. It also struck down the ban because it did not contain a "health exception." This exception would allow doctors to perform partial-birth abortions when it was "safer" for the mother's health.

The dissenting Supreme Court justices criticized the court's new "health exception," because it would make the ban meaningless. If abortion doctors determine when the procedure is "necessary," then, they reasoned, no state could ever realistically enforce the ban.

Congress Passes a Defiant Federal Ban

Before *Stenberg*, Congress had joined the states in passing a federal partial-birth abortion ban. But President Clinton had vetoed it many times because it did not include a "health exception." With the election of George W. Bush in 2000, new hope rose that a federal ban could be achieved.

Guided by *Stenberg*, Congress rewrote its ban so that it would not apply to other "legal" methods of abortion. This had been a major defect, according to the court, in the unconstitutional Nebraska law. But Congress refused to add a "health exception" to the law. Instead, Congress took a gamble on a risky political strategy that pitted it directly against the Supreme Court.

After conducting numerous hearings, Congress concluded that the partial-birth abortion procedure was never medically necessary to preserve a mother's health; in fact, it found that the procedure posed serious health risks to the mother. With

Protecting Children Against Infanticide

Partial birth legislation operates at the borderline between prenatal and postnatal human life. As a consequence of *Roe v. Wade* [which made abortion legal], this border separates, in the eyes of the federal judiciary, human non-persons from human persons, and constitutional "rights" from legal wrongs. . . .

The central premise of the federal partial birth statute is the defense of the border against the encroachment of abortion into infanticide. What matters most to this specific defense is the protection of all children who, while still alive and therefore capable of being protected, break the plane that currently marks the dividing line between non-personhood and personhood, between abortion and infanticide. The label the abortionist uses for his lethal procedure is irrelevant. The reason for using this macabre method of killing is irrelevant. What is crucial is maintenance of the bulwark against infanticide.

American Center for Law and Justice,
Amicus Brief, December 8, 2004.
www.aclj.org.

these conclusions in hand, Congress defied the Supreme Court and passed a ban on partial-birth abortion that did not contain the "health exception" required by *Stenberg*. Congress reasoned that it was the job of the legislative branch to determine the true facts of complex issues. Traditionally courts have deferred to Congress's factual findings.

On Nov. 5, 2003, President Bush signed the federal partial-birth abortion ban, stating: "For years, a terrible form of violence has been directed against children who are inches from birth, while the law looked the other way. Today, at last, the American people and our government have confronted the violence and come to the defense of the innocent child."[1]

Less than a year later three federal courts have ruled that the ban is unconstitutional. Congress's risky strategy has turned into a tragic legal failure. The judges who recently struck down the ban did not give Congress the deference that its findings of fact had traditionally received. Instead, they viewed Congress's findings as self-contradictory and partially false. As a result, the partial-birth abortion ban is now in jeopardy. Although the government can appeal these recent decisions, it is unlikely that the Court of Appeals or the U.S. Supreme Court will treat the ban any better.

Reasons to Support the Ban

Supporters of the ban on partial-birth abortion have asserted two key reasons for banning the horrid procedure. First, they argue that the law prohibits a procedure that is more akin to infanticide than abortion. In his dissent from the *Stenberg* decision, Justice Anthony Kennedy explained why the ban is necessary. He wrote: "States also have an interest in forbidding medical procedures which . . . cause the medical profession or society as a whole to become insensitive, even disdainful, to life. . . . " Partial birth abortion is different from other abortion methods because "the fetus is 'killed outside of the womb' where the fetus has an autonomy which separates it from the right of the woman to choose treatments for her own body."

Without the ban, the medical profession is on a slippery slope that makes it more acceptable to devalue human life and kill even those babies who are just inches from birth.

Pro-life activists also point to a second reason why the ban is so crucial. Experts have testified that partial-birth abortion causes "prolonged and excruciating pain" to unborn children.

---

1. On July 15, 2005, the 8th U.S. Circuit Court of Appeals ruled the Partial-Birth Abortion Ban Act of 2003 unconstitutional because it lacked an exception to preserve the health of the mother.

Studies have shown that during the middle stages of fetal growth an unborn child has a deeper sense of pain than the child will have after birth. Thus, the ban can spare innocent children the prolonged and severe pain associated with the procedure.

Does the Ban Really Protect Babies?

There are good reasons to support a ban on partial-birth abortion. But a closer look at the ban reveals that while it provides little protection for unborn children, its true value lies in its symbolic power.

As an initial concern, the ban regulates only one of several available methods of abortion during the second or third trimesters of pregnancy. In fact, the banned procedure is used in relatively few abortions. Statistics for partial-birth abortion range from as few as 640 to as many as 5,000 procedures out of the hundreds of thousands of abortions performed each year.

Congress went out of its way to ensure that the ban would not impede a woman from aborting her child using another "legal" abortion method. This was necessary because the current majority on the Supreme Court will not allow other abortion methods to be banned. That would pose an "undue burden" on a woman's "right" to an abortion, it argues. Ironically, targeting only a single method of abortion weakens the ban's justification. Justice Stevens—an abortion supporter— argued in *Stenberg* that it was "irrational" to regulate only one method of abortion because the other procedures are just as "gruesome" and disrespectful to "potential life." Justice Stevens has a point: the most common second-trimester abortion method (known as Dilation and Extraction, or D&E) involves literally ripping the unborn child apart limb from limb while the child is still living within the mother's womb.

The most sobering realization about the ban on partial-birth abortion is that it does not actually save the life of the unborn child. This was made distressingly clear during the recent New York challenge to the federal ban. Government lawyers defending the ban argued that a doctor could legally use the banned procedure as long as the baby was already dead during delivery. This would exploit a legal loophole that required that the child be alive during the procedure. A doctor could first kill the child by injecting potassium chloride or digoxin into the heart. Then, the doctor could—without violating the ban—continue with a partial-birth abortion in the same horrid manner as always.

There is only one benefit to the unborn child from using this offensive loophole. The child would be spared the prolonged and excruciating pain associated with undergoing the partial-birth abortion procedure. . . .

The Ban's True Power and Success

The partial-birth abortion ban is not perfect and provides only slight protection for unborn children. Yet despite its deficiency, the ban has succeeded in educating society and in swaying public opinion to help the unborn. The partial-birth abortion issue has kept the abortion debate at the forefront of the American conversation.

Periodical Bibliography

Shannen W. Coffin — "The Abortion Distortion," *National Review*, July 12, 2004.

Cynthia L. Cooper — "'Fetal Pain' Bill New Item on Anti-Choice Agenda," *WeNews*, August 16, 2004. www.womensenews.org.

David Crary — "In Abortion Debate, Mississippi Shows How Far a State Can Go with Array of Restrictions," Associated Press, December 22, 2004.

Ellen Goodman — "Abortion and the Age of Reason," *Boston Globe*, May 1, 2005.

John Langan — "Observations on Abortion and American Politics," *America*, October 25, 2004.

Mark R. Levin — "Death by Policy," *National Review*, March 14, 2005.

J. Peter Nixon — "The Other Half of the Story: Men and Abortion," *U.S. Catholic*, February 2005.

Tammy Smith — "Few Black Voices Heard on Abortion," *Richmond Times-Dispatch*, March 3, 2005.

Mary Zeiss Stange — "Guns, Like Abortion, Are a Matter of Choice," *USA Today*, May 5, 2004.

Richard W. Stevenson and Linda Greenhouse — "O'Connor, First Woman on High Court, Resigns After 24 Years," *New York Times*, July 1, 2005.

OPPOSING
VIEWPOINTS®
SERIES

CHAPTER 2

Is the Death Penalty Necessary?

Chapter Preface

Americans' support of the death penalty has varied widely in the nation's history. According to the Gallup Organization, American public opinion supporting the death penalty for persons convicted of murder ranged from a low of 42 percent in 1966 to a high of 80 percent in 1994. Such wide-ranging public opinion reflects changes in the level of violent crime in the nation and the influence of major religious organizations.

Stuart Banner's book *The Death Penalty: An American History* offers evidence showing how periods of high crime are correlated with greater approval of the death penalty. For example, in January 1920, when the enactment of the Eighteenth Amendment to the U.S. Constitution made the manufacture and sale of alcoholic beverages illegal, the booze business went underground and was soon dominated by gangsters. The result was a surge in violent crime during the era called Prohibition. The amendment was repealed in 1933, but public sentiment had already shifted to support the death penalty. The 199 death penalty executions in 1935 marked a record high for the nation.

Following World War II the country enjoyed a period of relative prosperity and lower crime rates. Gallup polls recorded a low of 42 percent support for the death penalty in May 1966, and there were no executions in the following year. In 1972 the U.S. Supreme Court struck down all state death penalty laws. At the same time, a renewed surge in violent crime brought public demand for action. By 1976 numerous states had enacted new death penalty laws, which the Court upheld. The high crime rates of the 1980s and 1990s resulted in high death penalty approval rates. According to the *Washington Post*, "Support for the death penalty hit 84 percent in one poll in the mid-1980s and stood at 80 percent as recently as 1994. Then it began to decline as crime rates dropped in the 1990s." A drop in homicides during the 1990s resulted in fewer death sentences and a decline in executions from 98 in 1999 to 60 in 2005. However, Gallup polls indicated continued high support for capital punishment. In May 2005 the organization reported that 74 percent of Americans surveyed favored the death penalty for persons convicted of murder.

The strong support of capital punishment today, despite relatively low crime rates, is anomalous. Such defense of capital punishment during a period of reduced crime may reflect the influence of religious organizations, particularly conservative Christians. In June 2000, for example, the powerful Southern Baptist Convention amended its statement of faith to support the death penalty for "those guilty of murder or treasonous acts that result in death." In making this decision leaders cited biblical references forbidding the taking of "innocent" human life as a basis for affirming the death penalty for individuals found guilty of capital crimes. To be sure, conservative Christians have enjoyed increasing political power, often acting through Congress and the presidency, both of which have been dominated by Republicans, who often favor the death penalty, since 2000.

This period of high support for capital punishment despite low crime rates is unusual in the nation's history. As has been shown, usually when crime escalates, citizens begin to get fearful, and their support of capital executions increases. The viewpoints in this chapter examine whether capital punishment does indeed deter crime. Authors also explore how Americans today feel about the death penalty, and whether juveniles who commit murder should be executed.

> *"Each execution deters other murders*
> *. . . with a best-estimate average of*
> *eighteen lives saved per execution."*

The Death Penalty
Deters Crime

Iain Murray

In the following viewpoint Iain Murray, an opponent of capital punishment on religious grounds, takes a critical look at research conducted by three Emory University economists. He concludes that they provide striking evidence that executions of murderers deter other murders and save lives. While he identifies some flaws in the research, he credits the researchers with overcoming problems that plagued earlier studies. Murray is a senior research analyst with the Statistical Assessment Service, a nonprofit, nonpartisan public policy organization based in Washington, D.C.

As you read, consider the following questions:

1. In determining the number of lives saved by each execution, the Emory University researchers calculated the

Iain Murray, "More Executions, Fewer Deaths," *American Outlook*, July/August, 2001.

effect of the murder rate on what factors?

2. What were some examples of "expected results" of the research, according to Murray?

3. What three results of the research did the author find odd?

Europe assails us as barbaric for embracing it. Churchmen worry for our immortal souls because we think that it is just. Governors lose sleep over the issue. It is the death penalty, and the debate over its imposition is now more intense than at any time since its brief suspension as unconstitutional in the 1970s. The federal executions of terrorist Timothy McVeigh and drug kingpin Juan Paul Garza, the first uses of the punishment by federal authorities since 1963, have intensified the arguments on both sides. European governments used the issue as a stick with which to beat President [George W.] Bush during his first visit to the Continent, and in Ohio, a group of religious-conservative lawmakers have stood up to oppose the penalty based on their religious faith.

In this atmosphere, death penalty proponents have found their arguments tested as never before. The contention that it is a just punishment is countered by the possibility that innocents have been executed. Although there is no proof that such a calamity has occurred since the restoration of the death penalty in 1976, its mere potential has been enough for some state governors to impose moratoria on executions. The argument that the penalty at least incapacitates the murderer himself and prevents him from murdering again has been attacked by life-imprisonment advocates as an overreaction. Murderers are the least likely of all criminals to repeat their crime, but it does occur. One notable recent case occurred in June 1999, when Leroy Schmitz, who served eleven years in a Massachusetts prison for strangling his girlfriend, murdered his wife in similar fashion in Montana. But for the most part, murderers who kill again have not been found guilty of capital murder and have never faced the death sentence.

The deterrent effect of execution, the argument that might serve death penalty proponents best, has had the worst time of all. A *USA Today* poll carried out in early June [2001], around the time of McVeigh's execution, found that 66 percent of respondents did not think that his death would serve as "a deterrent to future acts of violence and murder." Major figures in the debate, such as former governor of New York Mario Cuomo, point to cases such as that of Andrea Yates, who admitted slaying her five children, as evidence that many murders are irrational acts and therefore cannot be deterred. Others have argued that there are too few executions to have any deterrent effect. . . .

New Data Supports Deterrence

Until now, believers in the deterrence effect of executions have had little hard evidence with which to counter such straw man debating techniques. The work of economist Isaac Ehrlich of the State University of New York in the 1970s, which found a significant deterrent effect, had been diluted by constant reinvestigation and criticism. In the end, it suffered most from being out of date, as it was based on evidence from before the suspension of the death penalty in 1972. Its relevance to the modern debate was therefore questionable.

But there now come impressive new findings from a trio of economists at Emory University in Georgia. Hashem Dezhbakhsh, Paul Rubin, and Joanna Mehlhop Shepherd released their paper "Does Capital Punishment Have a Deterrent Effect? New Evidence from Post-Moratorium Panel Data" in January 2001. Its findings are striking. The authors conclude that each execution deters other murders to the extent of saving between eight and twenty-eight innocent lives, with a best-estimate average of eighteen lives saved per execution.

The researchers reached this conclusion scientifically, by expressing the murder rate mathematically. They calculated the effect on the murder rate of a number of factors including, specifically, the likelihood of being arrested, the chance of being sentenced to death after arrest, and the chance of being executed after sentence. They were then able to work out how significant the chance of being executed is to the murder rate. They found that executions themselves are a very significant factor, certainly much more so than the simple removal of the murderer from the pool of potential killers. And their findings pass all the statistical tests that show that it's not just by chance that the math works that way.

Methodology Is Critical to Acceptance of Research Results

This "econometric" method of looking at crime and other social phenomena is gaining popularity among researchers and has led to some controversial claims. Foremost among the econometricians is John Lott Jr., a research scholar at Yale, whose pioneering work on the effects on crime of issuing permits to carry concealed handguns has provoked a storm of controversy. Perhaps equally famous is the claim by the University of Chicago's Stephen Levitt and Stanford's John Donohue that the legalization of abortion in the early 1970s led to the drop in crime some twenty years later. Criminologist James Alan Fox of Northeastern University characterized Levitt and Donohue's work as "voodoo economics," while Lott's work has come under repeated fire for failing to control for numerous outside factors or for being circular in some way. Interestingly, Lott has answered all of his critics by continually refining his model, and has always obtained the same basic results. Nevertheless, his work and methodology continue to infuriate those who think they know better.

With these precedents in mind, it is important to look critically at the new work from Emory. The most obvious objection to the research is that it might fail to capture all the outside factors that feed the murder rate besides the criminal's rational assessment of his chances of getting caught. Factors such as drug trafficking, gun availability, and the overall supply of potentially violent young males are all recognized as important contributors to murder rates.

The researchers attempted to include these factors by constructing another element in their equation, taking account of crime rates for assault and robbery (which sometimes lead to murder), income levels, welfare levels, population density, six demographic categories for race and gender, and the state-level membership rate for the National Rifle Association (NRA), to serve as a proxy for gun ownership rates. They also took into account national-level trends such as the increasing amount of violence in America's popular culture. Finally, they added a variable to account for completely random factors. They then measured the results of their equations at both state and county levels, to give them as detailed a picture as possible. No earlier research, it is important to note, had ever gone into this level of detail.

Some Puzzles in Results

Most of the results they obtained were as expected. The murder rate increased as assault and robbery increased, and it also varied with the number of males in a county and with the proportion of African-Americans. It decreased according to the size of the non-African-American minority population. It also decreased with higher population density, which may at first sight seem strange, but it should be borne in mind that rural areas, with low population density, often have higher murder rates than the peaceful suburbs.

Three results do, however, appear rather odd. The first is that the murder rate appears to increase with per capita income. The researchers explain this by suggesting that drug consumption, which is heavily linked to murder, may increase

States with the Death Penalty

Alabama	Kentucky	Ohio
Arizona	Louisiana	Oklahoma
Arkansas	Maryland	Oregon
California	Mississippi	Pennsylvania
Colorado	Missouri	South Carolina
Connecticut	Montana	South Dakota
Delaware	Nebraska	Tennessee
Florida	Nevada	Texas
Georgia	New Hampshire	Utah
Idaho	New Jersey	Virginia
Indiana	New Mexico	Washington
Illinois	New York*	Wyoming
Kansas*	North Carolina	

(Also: U.S. Government and U.S. Military)

* Statutes were declared unconstitutional in 2004.

States Without the Death Penalty

Alaska	Massachusetts	Rhode Island
Hawaii	Michigan	Vermont
Iowa	Minnesota	West Virginia
Maine	North Dakota	Wisconsin

(Also: District of Columbia)

SOURCE: Death Penalty Information Center, June 2005.

along with income. This is, however, speculation. The researchers did not include a true measure of drug consumption or trafficking in their equation, which is probably the biggest single mark against it. If, however, the researchers' assumption is true, it appears that the metropolitan elite's habit of purchasing drugs as a recreational luxury is contributing to the murder rate. This is not an argument that is often made in considering how the war against drugs should be fought, but it does provide food for thought.

Another seemingly odd result is that a higher percentage of the population being teenage seems to lower the murder rate. This is again surprising, as the teen murder rate is the one that showed the biggest increase during the 1990s. It may be, however, that higher teenage populations involve proportionally more teenage girls, who are much less likely to murder than boys. Furthermore, the prime age for murder remains the immediate post-teen years, and it may be the size of *that* category that is most important. Unfortunately, the demographic category the researchers used was of ages twenty through twenty-nine, which includes large numbers who are putting their risky pasts behind them.

The final odd result was that the size of the state's NRA membership seems to increase the murder rate. This cannot be an effect of the murder rate rather than a cause, because the researchers took time lags into account in their models. NRA membership may, however, be a good indicator of the violence potential in a state, as states that have been previously more inclined to violence during earlier crime cycles retain high membership rates. States that have no real history of murder, however, may have fewer NRA members, as there is less need to join for self-protective purposes.

Deadly Implications

Despite all these reasonable explanations for the few odd results, the latter create enough doubt to cause one to worry about the robustness, if not the direction, of the authors' overall conclusion about deterrence. As mentioned earlier, one of the strengths of John Lott's work on guns is that the continued attacks by opponents of his view have resulted in continuous reassessment that has confirmed and thereby strengthened his original conclusions. His original paper was reworked into a book, *More Guns, Less Crime*, in 1998, which was updated again with a second edition, in 2000. Perhaps the best thing to happen to this research on capital punishment would be for the opponents of the death penalty to attack the assumptions and modeling techniques on which the findings rely. The researchers would then be forced to refine their model to rebut the attacks, by, for instance, including a measure of drug trafficking offenses or the like in the equation. If the conclusions still held true after such refinements, then the argument would be bolstered further.

In a way, this research is already a refinement and updating of Ehrlich's earlier work. It seeks, for instance, to answer the Cuomo argument that not all murders are rational, by estimating the number of murders that are unpreventable by deterrence and controlling for that factor. Similarly, the use of data collected since the restoration of the death penalty makes the research reasonably up-to-date. The use of county-level data avoids the problem that arises from using only national-level data, that of being unable to assess the true effects of individual states' policies. By any measure, this study is already a hugely important contribution to the debate.

Which makes one wonder why it has not received the publicity it should have. A search of the Lexis-Nexis news database reveals that the story has only been covered in the Washington insiders' magazine *The National Journal* and in a brief news item on Fox News' *Special Report with Brit Hume*. Without wishing to speculate, one might surmise that death penalty opponents saw how quickly John Lott's work entered the national consciousness once gun control proponents attacked it, and hoped to avoid such a boomerang effect. . . . Moreover, in contrast to the cases of gun control and abortion, which have strong advocacy groups such as the NRA and the various pro-choice groups arguing over them, there is no big pro-death penalty organization eager to spread the word about this new research.

Striking Implications

But the implications are huge. By the study's estimate, the two recent federal executions will save approximately thirty-six lives. On the final day of 1999 (the last day for which we have accurate figures), there were 3,527 prisoners under sentence of death in American prisons. This study suggests that if all those sentences were carried out *63,000 lives* would be saved. There were approximately 15,000 homicides in America in 1999, meaning that the deterrence effect could be the equivalent of four years free from murder. Even the most committed opponents of the death penalty should take notice of that figure.

"Statistical attempts to evaluate the worth of the death penalty as a deterrent . . . have occasioned a great deal of debate. The results simply have been inconclusive."

The Death Penalty Does Not Deter Crime

Robert Grant

Robert Grant asserts in the following viewpoint that capital punishment fails as a deterrent. He asserts that violence breeds more violence, and since capital punishment is a violent revenge, it breeds greater crime. He argues for more effective police investigations, rehabilitation of offenders, and life without parole as alternative to the death penalty. Grant is an attorney and former judge who teaches American government at Augusta State University in Georgia. This viewpoint originally appeared in his book American Ethics and the Virtuous Citizen: The Right to Life.

As you read, consider the following questions:

Robert Grant, "Capital Punishment and Violence," *The Humanist*, vol. 64, January/February, 2004, pp. 25–29. Copyright © 2004 by the American Humanist Association. Reproduced by permission of the author.

1. What region of the United States accounted for the majority of executions between 1977 and 2002, as reported by Grant?
2. According to the author, what is the one true reason for demanding death over life imprisonment?
3. What is the meaning of "restorative justice," as the author uses it?

Many in U.S. society demand vengeance and retribution for violent criminal conduct. Retributive justice means that the criminal must be made to pay for the crime by a crude mathematics that demands the scales of justice be balanced; this appeals to humanity's basest animal instincts and ancient demands for an eye for an eye, a life for a life. Retributive justice is fueled by hatred and satisfied only with full and complete revenge—the more cruel, the more satisfying. Civil liberties defender and lawyer Clarence Darrow observed that the state "continues to kill its victims, not so much to defend society against them . . . but to appease the mob's emotions of hatred and revenge." After Oklahoma City bomber Timothy McVeigh was executed amid wide television coverage, over 80 percent of the viewers polled said that he deserved to die; many said his death was too clinical and he should have died more painfully. One man said that McVeigh should have been stoned to death. Others were willing to forgo his execution because they thought that life behind bars with no possibility of parole would be a greater punishment.

Retributive justice has a bad history, however, as it has historically been used to enforce a class society by oppressing the poor and protecting the rich. It has been used to impose racism by applying the law in an unfairly heavy-handed way upon African-American citizens and in a lenient manner upon white Americans. The U.S. justice system has imprisoned more that two million people; about half are black, although African-Americans constitute only 12 percent of the total population. The prison system has been likened to a twenty-first century form of slavery.

Execution Statistics Show Capital Punishment Most Frequent in the South

More astonishing, perhaps, is that execution statistics from 1977 through 2002 show that capital punishment isn't so much a national problem as it is a problem local to the South. Nationally, 563 executions occurred during this period and the eleven states of the old Confederacy account for about 87.5 percent of these. Texas is way ahead of the pack, having performed about one-third of all executions. In 2002 Texas alone killed thirty-three death row prisoners. It's no coincidence that the South is also the most violent region of the country. However as more and more death row prisoners in other states exhaust their appeals, capital punishment will become more of a national problem.

Of those who favor capital punishment, not all would agree that retribution is their motive. Many argue that it is a deterrent to murder. But is it? Think of the troubled boys at Columbine High School who killed a teacher and students first and then committed suicide. Many violent people— particularly violent adolescents—resort to violence toward others only as an alternative to suicide and, in many cases, kill themselves anyway after killing others. Capital punishment wouldn't be a deterrent to them.

If these might be viewed as exceptional circumstances, then a way of covering all circumstances would be to compare statistics between states and nations with and without capital punishment. However, the majority of the justices in [*Gregg v. Georgia* in which the Supreme Court decided capital punishment was not unconstitutional by itself], after reviewing the evidence, concluded, "Statistical attempts to evaluate the worth of the death penalty as a deterrent to crimes by potential offenders have occasioned a great deal of debate. The results simply have been inconclusive." This may be because whatever deterrence factor exists for capital punishment probably exists almost equally for life imprisonment.

Improved Police Investigations Needed

A far greater deterrent than either, however, would be more efficient police investigation. An average of twenty-two thousand murders and non-negligent manslaughters are committed annually in the United States but only two-thirds, or fifteen thousand, suspects are arrested. And only 45 percent, or about ten thousand, of all accused killers are convicted.

So, in the end, there is only one purpose, one motive, one true reason for demanding death over life imprisonment: revenge. The issue isn't whether the state has the right to execute those who commit premeditated murder; it has. The issue is whether the state *ought* to execute convicted murderers.

The U.S. justice system has reverted to a strictly punitive method in order to prove "tough on crime" and in the hope that stronger punishment will somehow deter future criminal activity. But the reality is that severe punishment isn't working. Kids and petty offenders under the current system become hardened, violent, and persistent criminals. The present punitive and retaliatory justice system is unworthy of the American people's high standard of justice, which values the individual and demands equal justice for all.

Some Argue that Capital Punishment Breeds Violence

Many who seek to eliminate the culture of violence in society assert that capital punishment actually exacerbates the level and intensity of violence in the community. They observe that the state is backwardly killing people in order to teach others not to kill. They search for ways to heal the effects of crime upon society, the victim, and the offender. Restorative justice seeks to eliminate violence from the community and heal the harm done to the extent possible.

Violence is a highly contagious social disease that causes emotional, psychological, and physical damage and turns a peaceful person into a hostile one. The essence of violence is hatred, anger, rage, and desire for revenge caused by an act of wrongful violence internalized by the victim. When one allows oneself to be filled with these emotions in response to a violent attack, it allows the attacker to do more than just cause physical injuries. The attacker then does emotional and psychological damage as well. She or he has destroyed the victim's sense of inner tranquility and stability—a destruction that remains long after the physical injuries have healed. When anger, rage, hatred, and vengeance fill that space, the victim is turned from a peaceful to a violent person. This violence is the self-inflicted destruction of one's inner peace.

And violence begets more violence. It is a contagion spreading hatred, anger, rage, and desire for revenge to others out of empathy for the victim. Moreover, a violent victim may seek revenge against the original perpetrator and can be tempted to take out that anger on family members and friends when emotional triggers enflame the violent condition. Violent people don't have ample social skills to resolve differences peacefully and thus the contagion spreads. Each time a person commits a violent act with the intent to injure or kill, the attacker not only causes physical, emotional, and psychological injury to the victim but becomes a more violent person as well. Every act of violence makes the perpetrator more violent—whether the person is someone assaulting an innocent shopkeeper, acting in self-defense, performing a state execution, or soldiering in war. The contagious nature of violence infects the morally righteous police officer as well as the brutal lawbreaker. In his study of young murderers, Cornell University human development professor James Garbarino observes:

Trevor. Reproduced by permission.

Epidemics tend to start among the most vulnerable segments of the population and then work their way outward, like ripples in a pond. These vulnerable populations don't cause the epidemic. Rather, their disadvantaged position makes them a good host for the infection. . . . The same epidemic model describes what is happening with boys who kill.

Horrifically, this is a social disorder that can turn innocent people against each other.

Resisting Violence

A productive way to react to an act of violence is to have the courage to resist the normal impulse for revenge and punishment, to refrain from allowing anger, hatred, rage, and vengeance to destroy one's inner peace. Civil rights activist Martin Luther King Jr. observed:

> Returning violence for violence only multiplies violence, adding deeper darkness to a night already devoid of stars. Darkness cannot drive out darkness, only light can do that. Hate cannot drive out hate; only love can do that.

On the day of McVeigh's execution, a pastor at a memorial service for some of the victims' families asked, "Is there another way we can respond to this violence without doing violence ourselves?" Restorative justice doesn't promote anger, hatred, rage, or revenge by society or by the victim but offers a nonviolent response to the violence done. The focus of restorative justice isn't the punishment of the offender; it is the separation of the violent person from peaceful society for the protection of law-abiding citizens. With a peaceful attitude and conscious decision to choose a nonviolent and nonvengeful response, the cycle of violence can be broken and the contagion stopped. It is all a matter of attitude and the realization that violence should be countered in a mature and rational manner in order to protect society without doing damage to its citizens.

Treating Capital Punishment as a Disease

So we need to approach the problem of capital punishment not as a legal matter determining the rights and duties of the parties but as if we were treating a disease—the disease of violence. The past one hundred years have comprised the most violent century in human history. That violence is reflected in our television programs, movies, video games, literature, political attitudes, militaristic paranoia, the alarming abuse toward children, pervasive domestic violence, hostility toward the genuinely poor and helpless, the persistence of racism and intolerance, the way we treat petty juvenile offenders, and the mistreatment of prisoners. When we impose severe and excessive punishment, when we seek an eye for an eye, a tooth for a tooth, a life for a life, when we seek revenge on lawbreakers by some clumsy arithmetic we call justice, we become violent law abiders. We become what we say we abhor—more like criminals—more violent people. And the contagion spreads.

Every time we send a criminal to jail, especially a juvenile offender, it is a failure of society; every time that we execute a murderer, it is another failure of society. Where were the caring family members, helpful friends, concerned teachers, and supportive social workers when that criminal was a child being abused and neglected? Who loved that child? Who educated that child so that he or she could succeed in this world? Who demeaned that child because his or her skin color or religion or ethnicity was different from the majority in the community? Who did violence to that child by relegating him or her to poverty and then hating that child because he or she was poor? Generally speaking, children who are loved and cared for don't become criminals. Family and community violence toward children, including top-down governmental violence, turns some of them into criminals. Ethical communities don't need a police officer on every street corner because ethical communities care for all their children. Criminals aren't born; they are made.

And once made, society gives little thought to rehabilitating the offender, since the purpose of retributive justice is to punish. Or they view punishment as itself rehabilitative. Americans pretend that state-inflicted cruelty will somehow teach a violent felon *not* to be cruel and violent; and then 97 percent of these "rehabilitated" violent criminals are released into civil society. The theory seems to be that punishment teaches one how to become a good and respected member of the community. Yet the current punishments only succeed in destroying an offender's self-esteem by imprisoning that person and separating him or her from family and friends, then dehumanizing the prisoner by referring to him or her by a number instead of a name. Prisoners also become victims of the internal violence of prison life and, when not building up resentments, become schooled by other inmates in the techniques of crime—aware that society's rejection will continue once they are released.

In order to foster a less violent society, the treatment of the offender should be as humane and non-violent as forcible incarceration can allow. Rehabilitation of the offender ought to be a necessary condition of parole. Life imprisonment without the possibility of parole ought to be the alternative to capital punishment.

"*The May 2–5, 2005, Gallup Poll finds 74% of Americans saying they favor the death penalty for a person convicted of murder.*"

Americans Support the Death Penalty

Jeffrey M. Jones

In the following viewpoint, summarizing the results of a public opinion survey conducted May 2–5, 2005, Jeffrey M. Jones, managing editor with the Gallup Organization, finds increasing public support for the death penalty. He reports an increase since May 2004 in people who support the death penalty in murder cases, who prefer the death penalty over life imprisonment as punishment for murder, and who believe the death penalty is fairly applied. The survey used a national sample of 1,005 adults, aged eighteen and older.

As you read, consider the following questions:

1. The Gallup Organization has asked Americans if they favor the death penalty for persons convicted of murder

since what year?

2. Are men or women more strongly in favor of the death penalty, as cited by Jones?

3. According to Jones, do the majority of Americans believe executions of innocent people are frequent or rare?

Gallup's annual Moral Values and Beliefs poll finds that Americans are more positive in their orientation toward the death penalty than they have been in the past several years. Across a wide range of questions on the topic, Americans show a slight but noticeable increase in death penalty support. Compared with a year ago, more Americans say they support the death penalty as punishment for murder, more choose it over life imprisonment as the preferred punishment for murder, and more Americans believe the death penalty is applied fairly in this country.

Additionally, a majority of Americans now say the death penalty is not imposed often enough. There has also been a significant decline since 2003 in the percentage who believe that innocent people have been executed under the death penalty in the past five years. The increase in support for the death penalty is apparent across most societal subgroups.

Basic Support for the Death Penalty

The May 2–5, 2005, Gallup Poll finds 74% of Americans saying they favor the death penalty for a person convicted of murder, while 23% are not in favor. That represents a recent high in support, tied with a 74% reading in May 2003. Gallup has asked this version of the death penalty question since 1936, with a high water mark in support of 80% in 1994, and a low of 42% in 1966.

A second question on death penalty support—asking respondents whether the death penalty or life imprisonment with no possibility of parole is the better penalty for murder—

also shows an increase in pro-death penalty sentiment. Fifty-six percent of Americans say the death penalty is the better punishment, while 39% choose life imprisonment. The last time support for the death penalty was this high was in 1999, when 56% also said they preferred that option. The highest support for the death penalty that Gallup has measured on this question (dating back to 1985) was 61% in August 1997.

By a nearly two-to-one margin, men say they prefer the death penalty (65%) to life imprisonment (33%). Women, however, are about equally divided in their views, with 47% preferring the death penalty and 46% life imprisonment. This gender gap has been evident in previous years, but both groups are more likely to favor the death penalty this year than in the past.

Consistent with their basic support for the use of the death penalty, 70% of Americans say it is "morally acceptable," while 25% say it is "morally wrong." From 2001–2004, a lower percentage of Americans—between 63% and 65%—considered the death penalty morally acceptable.

Application of the Death Penalty

For the first time since Gallup began asking about the application of the death penalty in 2001, a majority of Americans say the death penalty is not imposed often enough. Fifty-three percent hold this view, while 24% say it is imposed the right amount of time, and 20% say it is imposed too often. Last year [2004], 48% said the death penalty was not imposed often enough, 25% the right amount of time, and 23% too often. In 2001, public opinion on this matter was very different. At that time, just 38% said the death penalty was not used enough, 34% said the right amount of time, and 21% too often.

Sixty-one percent say that, generally speaking, the death penalty is applied fairly in the United States today, while 35%

Death Row Inmates by State (October 1, 2004)

California	638
Texas	455
Florida	384
Pennsylvania	232
Ohio	206
North Carolina	201
Alabama	199
Arizona	128
Georgia	114
Tennessee	108
Oklahoma	97
Louisiana	91
Nevada	86
South Carolina	74
Mississippi	69
Missouri	58
Arkansas	39
Indiana	37
Kentucky	35
U.S. Government	34
Oregon	31
Virginia	23
Idaho	20
Delaware	19
New Jersey	15
Washington	11
Utah	10
Illinois	9
Maryland	9
Connecticut	8
Kansas	7
Nebraska	7
U.S. Military	7
Montana	4
South Dakota	4
Colorado	3
New Mexico	2
New York	2
Wyoming	2
Total Death Row	**3,471**

SOURCE: Death Penalty Information Center, 2004.

say it is applied unfairly. In 2003, 60% also said the death penalty was applied fairly, but in other years the percentage has been in the low-to-mid 50% range.

One possible reason for the increase in support for the death penalty is a declining belief that innocent people are being executed. Gallup finds a significant decrease in the percentage of Americans who believe that, in the past five years, innocent people have been executed under the death penalty—from 73% in May 2003 to 59% this year.

At the beginning of the decade, several death row inmates whose cases were reopened were found to be not guilty of the crime for which they received the death penalty. This led the state of Illinois—where many of those cases occurred—to institute a moratorium on executions, which remains in effect today. Maryland also imposed a moratorium in 2002, which has since been lifted.

Most Americans believe that executions of innocent people are rare—two in three believe this has happened in 5% or fewer cases in the last five years, including one-third who say it has not happened at all. Only 6% believe it has happened in more than 20% of the cases—less than half the percentage who said this in 2003 (13%).

Variations in Death Penalty Support

In its long history of polling on the death penalty, Gallup has consistently found that different groups are more or less likely to favor the death penalty. Those differences are apparent this year, as well. The following table shows the percentage of each group who finds the death penalty morally acceptable, comparing it to last year and reporting any change. In general, most groups show a slight increase in death penalty support compared with last year.

To summarize the major differences in subgroup support:

Men are much more likely to find the death penalty morally acceptable than women.

Whites are more supportive of capital punishment than non-whites.

Those with a post-graduate education are slightly less supportive of the death penalty than people with lower levels of education.

Conservatives are much more likely to view the death penalty more morally acceptable than are liberals.

Likewise, Republicans are much more pro-death penalty than Democrats.

People who attend church or religious services on a regular basis are less likely to support the death penalty than those who seldom or never attend.

| "Public support for capital punishment
dropped to 50 percent [in 2004]."

Americans Oppose the Death Penalty

Anna Badkhen

In this viewpoint San Francisco Chronicle *staff writer Anna Badkhen claims that Americans are shifting their support away from the death penalty. She cites as evidence the reduced numbers of death sentences and executions in recent years, and the changing positions of two U.S. senators, Sam Brownback and Rick Santorum, both former death penalty supporters. Badkhen also notes public opinion polls that show declining support for the death penalty, particularly among Catholics and evangelical Christians.*

As you read, consider the following questions:

1. According to the author, public support for capital punishment dropped to 50 percent in 2004 from what level in 1994?

2. Why did the Houston, Texas, police chief request a

moratorium on executions, according to Badkhen?

3. As stated by the author, what group began a new campaign in 2005 to end the death penalty in the United States?

It started when Rick Santorum, a conservative Republican senator from Pennsylvania, announced . . . that he was questioning his once unyielding support for the death penalty.

Then Sen. Sam Brownback, an equally conservative Kansas Republican, chimed in, saying capital punishment contradicts the efforts to establish a "culture of life," a phrase that became prominent during the controversy over Terri Schiavo's fate [when family members battled in courts over removing her life support].

Neither lawmaker has suggested that the United States abandon the death penalty altogether—it should still be reserved for the "most horrific and heinous of crimes," Santorum said.

But the apparent change of heart from two of its unequivocal supporters illustrates a broader tendency.

Problems with the Death Penalty

"We've come to a new era in this issue," said Richard Dieter, head of the Death Penalty Information Center, a nonprofit group in Washington critical of the death penalty. "There is a sense that there are problems with the death penalty, that there's a need for reform."

With an increasing number of convictions reversed by DNA evidence, receding murder rates and the huge financial costs of putting people to death, public support for capital punishment dropped to 50 percent last year [2004] from 80 percent in 1994, according to a Gallup poll.

The numbers of executions and death sentences have almost halved in the past five years, according to figures supplied by the Death Penalty Information Center. Last year, 59 death row inmates were executed, down from 98 in 1999; December was the first month in a decade that passed without an execution.

Courts Limit the Death Penalty

There are other signs of the death penalty's decline. Last month [March 2005] the U.S. Supreme Court, in a 5-4 decision [*Roper v. Simmons*], ruled that it was unconstitutional to execute juveniles, or those who committed capital murder when they were juveniles.

New York's Court of Appeals, the state's highest court, declared the death penalty statute unconstitutional last year. A bill to reinstitute the death penalty, which was passed by the state Senate last month, is expected to fail a state Assembly committee vote scheduled for Tuesday [the bill was defeated on April 12, 2005].

In Texas, which led the nation with 23 executions last year, Houston Police Chief Harold Hurtt called for a moratorium on executions on cases from his county, Harris County, after the local police crime lab was declared unreliable.

"I think it would be very prudent for us as a criminal justice system to delay further executions until we have had time to review the evidence," Hurtt said last fall. Gov. Rick Perry has rejected Hurtt's call, despite similar appeals from state and local lawmakers.

A Political Leader Changes His Attitude

Even President [George W.] Bush, who signed off on 152 executions in his six years as Texas governor, called for "dramatically expanding" the use of DNA evidence in capital cases in his State of the Union address in January.

Bush also called for an increase of federal funding for defense lawyers, saying that "people on trial for their lives must have competent lawyers by their side."

Perhaps even more unexpected were the statements from Sens. Santorum and Brownback, who had both voted against

Support for the Death Penalty Is Declining

Public support for death penalty in 1976 67%
Public support for death penalty in 1997 75%
Public support for death penalty in 2000 64%

"Death Penalty Update," Issues and Controversies on File,
September 15, 2000.

measures in the mid-1990s that would have made it easier for death-row inmates to appeal their sentences.

"While I still believe that the death penalty has some value, I have seen that there are serious questions about its use, such as possible wrongful convictions," said Santorum, through a spokeswoman.

"Whereas before I was an unquestioning supporter, now I am inclined to urge more caution," added Santorum, who in 1994 voted against a proposal to replace the death penalty with life imprisonment.

Establishing a Culture of Life

Brownback was even bolder "If we're trying to establish a culture of life, it's difficult to have the state sponsoring executions," he told *U.S. News & World Report* this month. He also suggested that taxpayer funding for abortions and capital punishment should be eliminated. "My hope is that we form a left-right coalition on life," he said.

Brownback's comment indicates a potential broadening of the conservative "culture of life" agenda, which has been limited primarily to opposition to abortion, same-sex marriage and stem-cell research.

"One of the really interesting things about the movement against the death penalty is how diverse it is," said Brooke

Matschek, a spokeswoman for the Religious Organizing Against the Death Penalty Project, a Philadelphia-based activist organization. "People are starting to understand that it's not a perfect system."

Santorum, who is Catholic, first expressed his change of heart late last month, after the U.S. Conference of Catholic Bishops began a campaign to end the death penalty in the United States on the heels of a sharp decline in support for capital punishment among America's Catholics.

Polls Reflect Changes

According to a Zogby International poll of 1,000 Catholics in March, just 48 percent supported capital punishment—down from 68 percent in 1994. John Zogby, who heads the polling organization, called the difference "huge."

Among America's evangelical Christians, support has dwindled from 82 percent in 1996 to 59 percent in 2004, according to a survey by the Pew Forum on Religion & Public Life—although influential conservative evangelical groups, such as Colorado-based Focus on the Family, continue to back executions.

"There are still some contradictions with people who consider themselves pro-life but not when it comes to the death penalty," said Matschek.

Death Sentences and Executions Continue

Dieter, of the Death Penalty Information Center, noted that the majority of Americans still back the death penalty, and that death sentences and executions continue.

As of Jan. 1, there were 3,455 inmates on death row, according to the NAACP (National Association for the Advancement of Colored People) Legal Defense and Education Fund—81 more than 2003, the most recent year in which the Justice Department supplies figures. The increase can be traced in part to the rise in the number of inmates on federal death row.

Next month [May 2005], Connecticut is scheduled to carry out the first capital punishment in New England in more than four decades, executing serial killer and rapist Michael Ross [Ross was executed May 13, 2005]. Two weeks ago, the Connecticut House of Representatives voted down a bill that would have replaced the state's death penalty with life imprisonment without possibility of parole.

A similar bill failed Tuesday in the Texas Senate. Ohio executed seven inmates in 2004, up from three in 2003.

Juries from the liberal Bay Area imposed three separate death sentences in the space of a week in December, first against Scott Peterson for murdering his wife, Laci, then, a day later, against Stuart Alexander who killed three meat inspectors, and, three days after that against Glenn Taylor Helzer, who dismembered the five people he murdered.

Nevertheless, Dieter says he detects a fundamental shift of attitude about the punishment.

"Although the death penalty remains real and can pop up in different places," he said, "it doesn't seem that it's being universally embraced."

> "The age-based line drawn by the Court is indefensibly arbitrary—it quite likely will protect a number of offenders who are mature enough to deserve the death penalty."

The Death Penalty Should Apply to Juveniles

Sandra Day O'Connor

On March 1, 2005, the U.S. Supreme Court handed down a decision (Roper v. Simmons) that banned the execution of offenders who were under the age of eighteen when their crimes were committed. In the following viewpoint, taken from her dissenting opinion, Justice Sandra Day O'Connor argues that some juveniles are mature enough to understand the severity of their crimes and are therefore as culpable as adults are. Thus, she concludes, excluding all juveniles from the death penalty is wrong.

As you read, consider the following questions:

1. O'Connor cites three differences between adults and juveniles on which the court based its decision to

Sandra Day O'Connor, dissenting opinion in the Supreme Court case *Roper v. Simmons,* No. 03-633, 2005.

prohibit the death penalty for juveniles. What are they?

2. What actions on the part of Christopher Simmons does O'Connor cite as evidence that the murder of Shirley Crook was premeditated and that he considered the risk of punishment?

3. Who does the author suggest is best capable of assessing a defendant's immaturity, susceptibility to outside pressures, and understanding of the consequence of his actions?

The Court's decision today establishes a categorical rule forbidding the execution of any offender for any crime committed before his 18th birthday, no matter how deliberate, wanton, or cruel the offense. Neither the objective evidence of contemporary societal values, nor the Court's moral proportionality analysis, nor the two in tandem suffice to justify this ruling.

Although the Court finds support for its decision in the fact that a majority of the States now disallow capital punishment of 17-year-old offenders, it refrains from asserting that its holding is compelled by a genuine national consensus. Indeed, the evidence before us fails to demonstrate conclusively that any such consensus has emerged in the brief period since we upheld the constitutionality of this practice in *Stanford v. Kentucky* (1989).

Instead, the rule decreed by the Court rests, ultimately, on its independent moral judgment that death is a disproportionately severe punishment for any 17-year-old offender. I do not subscribe to this judgment. Adolescents *as a class* are undoubtedly less mature, and therefore less culpable for their misconduct, than adults. But the Court has adduced no evidence impeaching the seemingly reasonable conclusion reached by many state legislatures: that at least *some* 17-year-old murderers are sufficiently mature to deserve the death penalty in an appropriate case. Nor has it been shown that capital sentencing juries are incapable of accurately assessing a youthful defendant's maturity or of giving due weight to the mitigating characteristics associated with youth. . . .

Three Differences Between Adults and Juveniles

Seventeen-year-old murderers must be categorically exempted from capital punishment, the Court says, because they "cannot with reliability be classified among the worst offenders." That conclusion is premised on three perceived differences between "adults," who have already reached their 18th birthdays, and "juveniles," who have not. First, juveniles lack maturity and responsibility and are more reckless than adults. Second, juveniles are more vulnerable to outside influences because they have less control over their surroundings. And third, a juvenile's character is not as fully formed as that of an adult. Based on these characteristics, the Court determines that 17-year-old capital murderers are not as blameworthy as adults guilty of similar crimes; that 17-year-olds are less likely than adults to be deterred by the prospect of a death sentence; and that it is difficult to conclude that a 17-year-old who commits even the most heinous of crimes is "irretrievably depraved." The Court suggests that "a rare case might arise in which a juvenile offender has sufficient psychological maturity, and at the same time demonstrates sufficient depravity, to merit a sentence of death." However, the Court argues that a categorical age-based prohibition is justified as a prophylactic rule because "[t]he differences between juvenile and adult offenders are too marked and well understood to risk allowing a youthful person to receive the death penalty despite insufficient culpability." . . .

The Court adduces no evidence whatsoever in support of its sweeping conclusion that it is only in "rare" cases, if ever, that 17-year-old murderers are sufficiently mature and act with sufficient depravity to warrant the death penalty. The fact that juveniles are generally *less* culpable for their misconduct than adults does not necessarily mean that a 17-year-old murderer cannot be *sufficiently* culpable to merit the death penalty. At most, the Court's argument suggests that the average 17-year-old murderer is not as culpable as the average adult murderer. But an especially depraved juvenile offender may nevertheless be just as culpable as many adult offenders considered bad enough to deserve the death penalty. Similarly, the fact that the availability of the death penalty may be *less* likely to deter a juvenile from committing a capital crime does not imply that this threat cannot *effectively* deter some 17-year-olds from such an act. Surely there is an age below which no offender, no matter what his crime, can be deemed to have the cognitive or emotional maturity necessary to warrant the death penalty. But at least at the margins between adolescence and adulthood—and especially for 17-year-olds such as respondent—the relevant differences between "adults" and "juveniles" appear to be a matter of degree, rather than of kind. It follows that a legislature may reasonably conclude that at least *some* 17-year-olds can act with sufficient moral culpability, and can be sufficiently deterred by the threat of execution, that capital punishment may be warranted in an appropriate case.

Simmons' Crime

Indeed, this appears to be just such a case. Christopher Simmons' murder of Shirley Crook was premeditated, wanton, and cruel in the extreme. Well before he committed this crime, Simmons declared that he wanted to kill someone. On several occasions, he discussed with two friends (ages 15 and 16) his plan to burglarize a house and to murder the victim by tying the victim up and pushing him from a bridge. Simmons said they could "get away with it" because they were minors. In accord with this plan, Simmons and his 15-year-old accomplice broke into Mrs. Crook's home in the middle of the night, forced her from her bed, bound her, and drove her to a state park. There, they walked her to a railroad trestle spanning a river, "hog-tied" her with electrical cable, bound her face completely with duct tape, and pushed her, still alive, from the trestle. She drowned in the water below. One can scarcely imagine the terror that this woman must have suffered throughout the ordeal leading to her death. Whatever can be said about the comparative moral culpability of 17-year-olds as a general matter, Simmons' actions unquestionably reflect "'a consciousness materially more depraved' than that of . . . the average murderer." (quoting *Godfrey v. Georgia*, (1980). And Simmons' prediction that he could murder with impunity because he had not yet turned 18—though inaccurate— suggests that he *did* take into account the perceived risk of punishment in deciding whether to commit the crime. Based on this evidence, the sentencing jury certainly had reasonable grounds for concluding that, despite Simmons' youth, he "ha[d] sufficient psychological maturity" when he committed this horrific murder, and "at the same time demonstrate[d] sufficient depravity, to merit a sentence of death."

Chronological Age Not an Unfailing Measure

The Court's proportionality argument suffers from a second and closely related defect: It fails to establish that the differences in maturity between 17-year-olds and young "adults" are both universal enough and significant enough to justify a bright-line prophylactic rule against capital punishment of the former. The Court's analysis is premised on differences *in the aggregate* between juveniles and adults, which frequently do not hold true when comparing individuals. Although it may be that many 17-year-old murderers lack sufficient maturity to deserve the death penalty, some juvenile murderers may be quite mature. Chronological age is not an unfailing measure of psychological development, and common experience sug-

Not All Juveniles Are Alike

The Court and a majority of state legislatures have held that individual consideration is a constitutional requirement before sentencing one to death. The Court needs to abide by this requirement and not group juveniles together as a class based on age. Rather, it should recognize that juvenile defendants, even those in the same age group, are shaped by individual life experiences and therefore possess different levels of maturity and make different choices. Consequently, their decisions affect their moral responsibility for a crime.

Justice for All Alliance, "Amici Curiae Brief Before the Supreme Court of Missouri," 2004.

gests that many 17-year-olds are more mature than the average young "adult." In short, the class of offenders exempted from capital punishment by today's decision is too broad and too diverse to warrant a categorical prohibition. Indeed, the age-based line drawn by the Court is indefensibly arbitrary—it quite likely will protect a number of offenders who are mature enough to deserve the death penalty and may well leave vulnerable many who are not. . . .

Moreover, it defies common sense to suggest that 17-year-olds as a class are somehow equivalent to mentally retarded persons with regard to culpability or susceptibility to deterrence. Seventeen-year-olds may, on average, be less mature than adults, but that lesser maturity simply cannot be equated with the major, lifelong impairments suffered by the mentally retarded.[1]

1. In *Atkins v. Virginia* (2002) the Court barred the death penalty for the mentally retarded because they lacked the intellectual capacity to be deterred by the death penalty as a consequence of their actions.

Individual Sentencing Decisions Are More Appropriate

The proportionality issues raised by the Court clearly implicate Eighth Amendment concerns. But these concerns may properly be addressed not by means of an arbitrary, categorical age-based rule, but rather through individualized sentencing in which juries are required to give appropriate mitigating weight to the defendant's immaturity, his susceptibility to outside pressures, his cognizance of the consequences of his actions, and so forth. In that way the constitutional response can be tailored to the specific problem it is meant to remedy. The Eighth Amendment guards against the execution of those who are "insufficiently culpable," in significant part, by requiring sentencing that "reflect[s] a reasoned *moral* response to the defendant's background, character, and crime." *California v. Brown* (1987). Accordingly, the sentencer in a capital case must be permitted to give full effect to all constitutionally relevant mitigating evidence. A defendant's youth or immaturity is, of course, a paradigmatic example of such evidence.

Although the prosecutor's apparent attempt to use respondent's youth as an aggravating circumstance in this case is troubling, that conduct was never challenged with specificity in the lower courts and is not directly at issue here. As the Court itself suggests, such "overreaching" would best be addressed, if at all, through a more narrowly tailored remedy. The Court argues that sentencing juries cannot accurately evaluate a youthful offender's maturity or give appropriate weight to the mitigating characteristics related to youth. But, again, the Court presents no real evidence—and the record appears to contain none—supporting this claim. Perhaps more importantly, the Court fails to explain why this duty should be so different from, or so much more difficult than, that of assessing and giving proper effect to any other qualitative capital sentencing factor. I would not be so quick to conclude that the constitutional safeguards, the sentencing juries, and the trial judges upon which we place so much reliance in all capital cases are inadequate in this narrow context. . . .

Applicability of the Eighth Amendment

In determining whether the Eighth Amendment permits capital punishment of a particular offense or class of offenders, we must look to whether such punishment is consistent with contemporary standards of decency. We are obligated to weigh both the objective evidence of societal values and our own judgment as to whether death is an excessive sanction in the context at hand. In the instant case, the objective evidence is inconclusive; standing alone, it does not demonstrate that our society has repudiated capital punishment of 17-year-old offenders in all cases. Rather, the actions of the Nation's legislatures suggest that, although a clear and durable national consensus against this practice may in time emerge, that day has yet to arrive. By acting so soon after our decision in *Stanford*,[2] the Court both pre-empts the democratic debate through which genuine consensus might develop and simultaneously runs a considerable risk of inviting lower court reassessments of our Eighth Amendment precedents.

To be sure, the objective evidence supporting today's decision is similar to (though marginally weaker than) the evidence before the Court in *Atkins*. But *Atkins* could not have been decided as it was based solely on such evidence. Rather, the compelling proportionality argument against capital punishment of the mentally retarded played a decisive role in the Court's Eighth Amendment ruling. Moreover, the constitutional rule adopted in *Atkins* was tailored to this proportionality argument: It exempted from capital punishment a defined group of offenders whose proven impairments

2. In *Stanford v. Kentucky* (1989) the court held that execution of 16- or 17-year-old capital murderers did not violate the Eighth Amendment.

rendered it highly unlikely, and perhaps impossible, that they could act with the degree of culpability necessary to deserve death. And *Atkins* left to the States the development of mechanisms to determine which individual offenders fell within this class.

In the instant case, by contrast, the moral proportionality arguments against the juvenile death penalty fail to support the rule the Court adopts today. There is no question that "the chronological age of a minor is itself a relevant mitigating factor of great weight" (*Eddings*), and that sentencing juries must be given an opportunity carefully to consider a defendant's age and maturity in deciding whether to assess the death penalty. But the mitigating characteristics associated with youth do not justify an absolute age limit. A legislature can reasonably conclude, as many have, that some 17-year-old murderers are mature enough to deserve the death penalty in an appropriate case. And nothing in the record before us suggests that sentencing juries are so unable accurately to assess a 17-year-old defendant's maturity, or so incapable of giving proper weight to youth as a mitigating factor, that the Eighth Amendment requires the bright-line rule imposed today. In the end, the Court's flawed proportionality argument simply cannot bear the weight the Court would place upon it.

Lack of a Clear National Consensus

Reasonable minds can differ as to the minimum age at which commission of a serious crime should expose the defendant to the death penalty, if at all. Many jurisdictions have abolished capital punishment altogether, while many others have determined that even the most heinous crime, if committed before the age of 18, should not be punishable by death. Indeed, were my office that of a legislator, rather than a judge, then I, too, would be inclined to support legislation setting a minimum age of 18 in this context. But a significant number of States, including Missouri, have decided to make the death penalty potentially available for 17-year-old capital murderers such as respondent. Without a clearer showing that a genuine national consensus forbids the execution of such offenders, this Court should not substitute its own "inevitably subjective judgment" on how best to resolve this difficult moral question for the judgments of the Nation's democratically elected legislatures. See *Thompson, supra,* at 854 (O'CONNOR J., concurring in judgment). I respectfully dissent.

> *"Most teenagers sent to death row are poor, black, and likely to have been convicted of killing whites."*

The Death Penalty Should Not Apply to Juveniles

Sasha Abramsky

In this viewpoint Sasha Abramsky argues that American standards of decency have changed to favor prison terms over death for juveniles convicted of capital murder. Abramsky claims that new scientific evidence suggests that juveniles may have less impulse control than do adults, information that has resulted in less support for executing juvenile offenders. According to Abramsky, using the death penalty on juveniles is shameful. Abramsky is a freelance journalist and author of Hard Time Blues: How Politics Built a Prison Nation.

As you read, consider the following questions:

1. The author cites research by an Ohio Northern University law professor that indicates what groups of teenagers were most likely to end up on death row?

2. How many states have actually executed someone for crimes committed as a juvenile since the death penalty was reinstated in the United States in 1976, as cited by the author?

3. Experts once believed that development of the human brain was complete by age three or four. New research indicates that brain development continues until about what age, according to Abramsky?

Despite a judiciary increasingly dominated by conservative appointees, the federal courts have shown a heartening willingness to rein in the death penalty. In recent years, they have limited who is eligible and have placed other restrictions on states' arbitrary conduct. Two years ago [2002], the U.S. Supreme Court, by a vote of 6 to 3, halted the practice of executing mentally retarded prisoners, declaring it unconstitutional in *Atkins v. Virginia.*

Later this year [2004], the Court will hear arguments in *Roper v. Simmons,* a watershed case involving Christopher Simmons, a young man who had lived on Missouri's death row for close to a decade after being convicted of a particularly gruesome murder committed when he was 17 years old. But in 2003, the Missouri Supreme Court ruled that the juvenile death penalty violated the Eighth Amendment's prohibition on cruel and unusual punishment, and, when the state appealed, the U.S. Supreme Court agreed to take the case. Since then, juvenile executions across the country have been put on hold.

Most experts believe it will be impossible for the Court to avoid a decision barring the execution of juveniles when the justices make their ruling public sometime in 2005.[1] "All the measures are exceeded," says Adam Ortiz, who works on the

---

1. The Court ruled on March 1, 2005, to forbid execution of offenders who were under age 18 at the time they committed the crime.

issue for the American Bar Association. Ortiz is referring to the fact that the same "measures" the Court cited in barring execution of the mentally retarded—an inability to fully interpret events and a lack of complete moral culpability, for example—hold true for juveniles in light of the new scientific understanding of the adolescent brain.

A Shift Away from Capital Punishment

Together, these developments represent the biggest shift away from capital punishment since the practice was briefly abolished in this country between 1972 and 1976. "This is the cutting edge of the death-penalty-reform movement," says Richard Dieter, executive director of the Washington-based Death Penalty Information Center

It is also a remarkable turnaround from the prevailing view on the Supreme Court in the late 1980s. In two seminal cases—*Thompson v. Oklahoma* (1988) and *Stanford v. Kentucky* (1989)—the justices upheld the juvenile death penalty but left open the door to reexamine it if community norms, or "standards of decency," changed in the years to come.

Since then, the standards of decency have indeed changed. A moral consensus is emerging that holds out room for the eventual rehabilitation of teenage criminals, even those convicted of particularly brutal murders, or at the very least one that judges the actions of immature teenagers by a slightly different moral calculator than that used for mature adults; that recognizes new scientific evidence on how the adolescent brain functions; and that seeks to understand, if not excuse, why some adolescents are prone to acts of extreme violence. Perhaps in no other area of the criminal-justice system has there been such a dramatic shift of moral sensibilities in so short a time frame. Importantly, this view is also informed by troubling body of evidence—gathered by experts like Ohio Northern University law professor Victor Streib—indicating that far from being blind, justice is capricious: Most teenagers sent to death row are poor, black, and likely to have been convicted of killing whites.

Life Without Parole Favored for Juveniles

because of the above factors, Americans increasingly favor prison terms, including life without parole, over death for juveniles convicted of capital murder. Last year, only two people in the United States were sent to death row for crimes committed when they were minors, down from seven in 2000. Though the number of Americans executed for crimes committed when they were minors has always been tiny compared to the number of adults executed, the punishment finally "seems to be out of style and it seems to be disappearing," says Streib. "It's like an endangered species."

Today, 20 states permit the execution of someone convicted of a crime committed when he or she was younger than 18. Of these, the Death Penalty Information Center estimates that 12 currently have juvenile offenders on death row, all of them in the South except Arizona, Nevada, and Pennsylvania; Texas leads the field with 28 people awaiting execution for crimes committed when they were 17 years old. But a mere seven states have actually carried out such an execution since 1976. Florida, for example, hasn't put a juvenile offender to death since 1954; Arizona since 1934; and Alabama, which has 14 juvenile offenders on its death row and which allows teenagers as young as 16 to be executed, since 1961. In fact, 89 percent of Americans live in states that have not executed a juvenile in more than a decade, reflecting the fact that prosecutors are apparently reluctant to seek the death penalty against juveniles even in states where they can.

Executing Juveniles in Texas

Not surprisingly, the majority of the juvenile executions that have occurred have been in the single state of Texas (eight out of 13 since 1999), many of them resulting from convictions in the infamous "convict-'em-and-execute-'em" Harris County.

Yet when Texas geared up two years ago to execute Napoleon Beazley, an African American convicted of killing a white man during a botched carjacking in 1994 when the former was 17 years old, 18 state legislators spoke out against the execution, and Judge Cynthia Kent, who had presided over Beazley's trial, wrote a letter to Governor Rick Perry urging him to commute the sentence. Professional organizations such as the American Bar Association and the American Psychiatric Association called for a halt to such killings, pointing out that only four countries worldwide—Congo, Iran, Pakistan, and the United States—acknowledge having executed juveniles in the years since 2000.

Ultimately unsuccessful, the campaign gathered steam even after Beazley was put to death by lethal injection. Newspapers across the country and human-rights organizations around the world declared his execution a travesty. An array of Nobel Peace Prize winners—including Jody Williams, Desmond Tutu, F.W. de Klerk, and the Dalai Lama—signed an open letter in Paris urging the United States to end these judicial killings. And back home in Texas, widespread opprobrium moved state senators to vote to ban the juvenile death penalty. The House failed to follow suit only after the governor intervened in support of preserving such executions.

Perry's action, however, did not dampen the national sentiment against the juvenile death penalty. In the years prior to Beazley's execution, Montana and Indiana had passed laws banning juvenile executions. Since Perry's intervention, South Dakota and Wyoming have also barred the punishment. And just before Christmas of last year, defenders of the juvenile death penalty received yet another setback, this time in Virginia. In one of the highest-profile capital-murder cases of recent times, a jury recommended not to impose the death penalty on Lee Boyd Malvo, the teenage triggerman in the notorious Washington, D.C., sniper killings. What made the decision all the more improbable was the fact that Attorney

Adolescents Are Less Responsible than Adults

America's justice system punishes offenders according to their culpability. Adolescents simply do not have the maturity of adults and are therefore less responsible than adults who commit similar crimes.

This same reasoning has led us to enact laws prohibiting individuals under 18 years of age from entering into contracts, making medical decisions, purchasing cigarettes, consuming alcohol, and voting.

Rosalyn Carter, Kentucky Herald-Leader, *February 11, 2003.*

General John Ashcroft had gone out of his way to secure a trial in Virginia precisely because Virginia juries were more likely to vote for death in cases where the defendant was a minor at the time the crimes occurred. Weeks earlier, another Virginia jury had elected to sentence adult sniper John Allen Muhammad to death for the killing spree.

Growing Consensus Opposes Executing Juveniles

The Virginia verdicts appear to reflect a broader view borne out by national opinion polls and studies of jurors in other capital cases: While a majority of Americans continue to support capital punishment for adults, a broad-based consensus is developing against the practice of executing juveniles.

Those few who defend the practice increasingly resort to a language of unilateralism, displaying paranoid hostility to perceived international encroachments on U. S. sovereignty. In September 2001, for example, during Beazley's appeals process, the state of Texas claimed that a move to bar juvenile executions would amount to bowing to "economic extortion from some European council," and that it would represent "social engineering by those who cannot achieve their neo-socialist designs on government through the democratic processes established in our state and federal constitutions."

Other proponents of juvenile capital punishment seem to long for a simpler world easily divided into . . . goods and evils. "If they're old enough to serve in the armed forces, they're old enough to be held accountable for capital crimes," says 48-year-old Austin attorney and former Marine William "Rusty" Hubbarth, of the Texas-based Justice for All organization. "If the government feels a 17-year-old is mature enough to be trained to be a professional killer, they're old enough to know the difference between right and wrong." Hubbarth, who opaquely states that his own family was the subject of a violent crime and who used to write case summaries for the Texas Board of Pardons and Paroles during presentations arguing for clemency for death-row inmates, adds, "Some of these people don't deserve to be breathing the same air as me."

Yet more and more, voices like Hubbarth's are the minority. Recent research by criminologists from Northeastern University's Capital Jury Project and the University of Delaware found that barely 18 percent of juries recommended the death penalty when a capital defendant was younger than 18 at the time of his or her crime. When the defendant was 18, only 34 percent of juries imposed a death sentence. But when a defendant was older than 18, between 55 percent and 65 percent of juries handed down death sentences. Reflecting a similar sensibility, a 2001 Texas poll found that only 34 percent of Lone Star State residents supported the juvenile death penalty, despite Texas' status as the nation's execution epicenter. And in 2002, a national Gallup Poll estimated that barely a quarter of all Americans favored the penalty for minors.

New Studies of the Adolescent Brain

To be sure, strong public unease with the juvenile death penalty has to do with a cultural reluctance to sanction the killing of children that has operated throughout American history. But more recent shifts in public opinion may be informed by advances in brain-imaging techniques and scientists' understanding of how the adolescent brain works.

In the 1960s, Harvard neurologist Paul Ivan Yakovlev began using a new staining technique on a collection of more than 1,500 brains from deceased people of various ages. His aim was to study how the brain continues to acquire fatty insulation, or myelin, as it ages through childhood and adolescence. The insulation facilitates the brain's ability to transmit information; to understand the past, present, and future; and to interpret its surroundings. Absent such insulation, the brain is restricted in how well it can interpret complex data and self-censor basic impulses—including violent ones. Yakovlev's findings, contradicting earlier theories, indicated that brain structures continue to evolve well beyond childhood.

"We used to think brain development was complete by 3 or 4 years old," explains David Fassler, trustee-at-large of the American Psychiatric Association and clinical professor of psychiatry at the University of Vermont. "We now know it continues through adolescence, and in some areas, even into early adulthood."

Technology Assists the Study of Brain Development

With more recent advances in magnetic resonance imaging, brain scans on living subjects have become far more sophisticated, allowing neuroscientists to develop detailed maps of how the brain changes over time, which parts of the brain change first, and which parts mature only in early adulthood.

"Until you are 18, the brain is changing," explains Ruben Gur, a neuropsychologist at the University of Pennsylvania

Medical School. "And those parts of the brain that come on board last, that myelinate last, are exactly those part of the brain that do the functions considered to be related to criminal culpability. The last parts of the brain to become myelinated are the frontal lobes and cortexes—the thinking parts of the brain."

For the vast majority of children, a good social network, parental advice, and the presence of teachers, mentors, and minders serve as a sort of societal substitute for the functions of the fully developed frontal cortex. In some children, however, that substitute is so absent or twisted—through neglect or abuse—that the child has no inhibitors to extreme acts of violence. Overwhelmingly, say neuropsychologists, these are the young people who are most at risk of ending up on death row. That doesn't mean that such children shouldn't be punished—and, when necessary, incarcerated for long periods—in order to protect society from their violent actions. What it does mean, however, is that complicating factors may exist that should be given serious weight during the sentencing phase of any capital case involving a juvenile.

Adolescent Executions Are a Shameful Mistake

Whether because of new scientific understandings or because of a greater communal sensitivity to the challenges faced by abused, disturbed young people, someday soon the juvenile death penalty may be a sorrowful anachronism, as antithetical to American values of fairness and justice as the burning of witches seems today.

Hours before Napoleon Beazley died in Texas's execution chamber, he released his final statement. "The act I committed to put me here was not just heinous, it was senseless," the condemned man wrote, his appeals all used up, his time on earth galloping away. "But the person that committed that act is no longer here—I am. I'm not going to struggle physically against any restraints. I'm not going to shout, use profanity or make idle threats. Understand though that I'm not only upset, but I'm saddened by what is happening here tonight. I'm not only saddened, but disappointed that a system that is supposed to protect and uphold what is just and right can be so much like me when I made the same shameful mistake."

When it comes to the death penalty, America has shown a peculiar propensity over the years for perpetuating the "Shameful mistake." . . . Once people see that justice can still be served without executing young criminals, perhaps they will be more inclined to believe that the justice system would still function were the death penalty as a whole consigned to history.

Periodical Bibliography

Scotty Ballard   "Should the Death Penalty Be Abolished?" *Jet*, February 24, 2003.

Bruce Bower   "Teen Brains on Trial: The Science of Neural Development Tangles with the Juvenile Death Penalty," *Science News*, May 8, 2004.

Robert H. Bork   "Travesty Time, Again: In Its Death-Penalty Decision, the Supreme Court Hits a New Low," *National Review*, March 28, 2005.

Cathleen Burnett   "Political and Societal Views on the Death Penalty," *Human Quest*, March/April 2003.

Christian Networks Journal   "Shalt Thou Kill?: An in-Depth Look at Capital Punishment," Fall 2005.

James D. Davidson   "What Catholics Believe About Abortion and the Death Penalty," *National Catholic Reporter*, September 30, 2005.

Kenneth Jost   "Death Penalty Controversies," *CQ Researcher*, September 23, 2005.

Robert Grant   "Capital Punishment and Violence," *Humanist*, January/February 2004.

Robert Rinearson   "Death Penalty Favors Victims over the Thugs Who Kill Them," *Fort Wayne News-Sentinel*, January 6, 2006.

Austin Sarat   "Schwarzenegger's Mistake: Clemency and Tookie Williams," *Jurist*, December 27, 2005.

OPPOSING VIEWPOINTS® SERIES

CHAPTER 3

What Factors Contribute to Teen Suicide?

Chapter Preface

Suicide is a uniquely teenage problem. According to the Centers for Disease Control and Prevention (CDC), suicide is the eighth leading cause of death of all U.S. residents, but it is the third leading cause of death among young people age 15 to 24. The report *Health, United States, 2005*, produced by the National Center for Health Statistics, tracked deaths by suicide from 1950 through 2002. The suicide death rate is reported as the number of deaths per 100,000 residents. In 1950 the suicide rate for all age groups was at a peak of 13.2 deaths per 100,000. By 2002 that rate had dropped to 10.9. However, between 1960 and 1990 deaths by suicide among young people ages 15 to 24 nearly quadrupled from 4.1 to 15.1.

According to the National Youth Risk Behavior Survey conducted by the Centers for Disease Control, in 2003, 16.9 percent of students in grades nine–twelve seriously considered suicide, 8.5 percent attempted suicide, and 2.9 percent required medical treatment as a result of suicide attempts. According to the study, female students were more likely to consider suicide (21.3 percent compared to 12.8 percent of male students), more likely to attempt suicide (11.5 percent compared to 5.4 percent of male students), and more likely to require medical care for suicide-related injuries (3.2 percent compared to 2.4 percent of male students). The highest rate of suicidal thoughts occurred in tenth grade for both female and male students.

As the adolescent suicide rate escalated in the second half of the twentieth century, researchers began to identify causal factors. Researcher A.L. Rosenkrantz, writing in 1978 for the magazine *Adolescence*, described the teen yeas as a time when

> ordinary levels of stress are heightened by physical, psychological, emotional, and social changes. . . . Adolescents suffer a feeling of loss for the childhood they must leave

behind, and undergo an arduous period of adjustment to their new adult identity. . . . Our achievement-oriented, highly competitive society puts pressure on teens to succeed, often forcing them to set unrealistically high personal expectations. . . . In an affluent society which emphasizes immediate rewards, adolescents are not taught to be tolerant of frustration.

Other researchers suggest that the state of the world, in which political turmoil is prevalent and sophisticated weapons of mass destruction threaten human existence, contribute to adolescents' sense of hopelessness. Many other factors contributing to teen suicide have been proposed as well. The Kids Health Web site identifies the following risk factors:

- the presence of a psychological disorder and alcohol and substance use;
- feelings of distress, irritability, or agitation;
- feelings of hopelessness and worthlessness resulting from experiences such as repeated failures at school, violence at home, or isolation from peers;
- a previous suicide attempt;
- a family history of depression or suicide;
- having suffered physical abuse or sexual abuse;
- lack of a support network, poor relationships with parents or peers, and feelings of social isolation; and,
- dealing with homosexuality in an unsupportive family or community or hostile school environment.

High teen suicide rates have prompted many researchers to try to discover what causes young people to attempt to end their lives. The viewpoints in this chapter consider three factors that may contribute to teen suicide: antidepressants, the availability of guns, and homosexuality. Researchers hope that by studying the problem, they can help save the lives of many teens struggling to find hope and happiness.

| *Antidepressants "increase the risk of suicide and hostility in children."*

Antidepressants Can Lead to Teen Suicide

Part I: Robert Fritz; Part II: Tom Woodward; Part III: Vera Sharav

The following three-part viewpoint consists of statements by three witnesses testifying before the U.S. Food and Drug Administration on February 2, 2004. Two witnesses are parents whose children committed suicide while taking antidepressants. The third is a resident of the Alliance for Human Research Protection. Due to the large number of public witnesses, statements were limited to two minutes each. The witnesses argue in this viewpoint that antidepressants have been shown to increase the risk of teen suicide, and they contend that the FDA has not adequately publicized the risk for fear of alienating U.S. drug companies.

As you read, consider the following questions:

1. What happened to Robert Fritz's daughter?

Robert Fritz, Tom Woodward, and Vera Sharav, "Testimony before the Food and Drug Administration Psychopharmacologic Drugs Advisory Committee and the Pediatric Subcommittee of the Anti-Infective Drugs Advisory Committee, Washington, DC," February 2, 2004. Reproduced by permission of the authors.

2. How did Tom Woodward's daughter kill herself, according to the viewpoint?

3. What did the FDA's Zoloft review find, as stated by Vera Sharav?

Part I

People have been pleading with the FDA [Food and Drug Administration] for 11-plus years to put warnings on prescriptions for antidepression medication to no avail. The FDA has had people present information about suicidal tendency increase and numerous completed suicides, and still no warnings of increased risk of suicide were issued. The people of the United States have a right to know what risks are associated with taking these drugs. I have a right to know what risks are associated with taking these drugs, so I can make an informed decision as to whether or not I want my children to take these drugs. The need for a warning is compounded by the fact that doctors are prescribing these medications off label. My daughter, Stephanie Raye Fritz, was taking Zoloft [a type of selective serotonin reuptake inhibitor (SSRI)]. We weren't told of any risk of increased suicidal tendencies or increased suicide attempts. She hung herself . . . in her bedroom after finishing her homework. She showed no signs of increased depression or imminent suicidal thoughts, and, in fact, was still recruiting people to see her sing the following month. We had no warning of what Zoloft could do to our daughter, but you people, the FDA, certainly did. . . . Two weeks before she took her life, you put out a Public Health Advisory and notified physicians about preliminary data from studies suggesting an excess of reported suicidal ideation and suicide attempts for pediatric patients receiving certain of these antidepressant drugs. Why weren't we, the parents of the kids taking Zoloft, notified with this advisory? It is too late for my daughter, but for the FDA to continue to sit on this information and not let the public know the risks associated with these drugs is a gross misuse of power. I am not asking that these drugs be taken off the market. I don't know enough about their safety to recommend that. What I am seeking is that when the drugs are prescribed off label, or when drugs are prescribed after an advisory is issued suggesting new adverse side effects, that the FDA make it mandatory that the physicians prescribing such drugs explain in plain English what the risks are and that an informed written consent be received from the parents or the patient's guardian. I hope that you will agree that all Americans deserve to know what risks they are assuming when they take medication. I believe that most Americans, including most elected officials, agree with that. How many more people have to die before a warning gets issued?

Part II

My name is Tom Woodward. My wife Kathy and I have been married for 19 years and until 6 months ago had 4 children. Our oldest child, Julie, hung herself after 7 days on Zoloft, and she was only 17, was a cautious child, and had no history of self-harm or suicide, nor was there any history of depression or suicide in our family. The doctors we spoke with stressed that Zoloft was safe and had very few side effects. The possibility of violence, self-harm, or suicidal acts was never raised. The two and a half pages we received with the Zoloft never mentioned self-harm or suicide. Julie began experiencing akathisia [extreme agitation and restlessness] almost immediately. We now know from a blood test from the coroner's office that she was not metabolizing the drug. We are 100 percent convinced that Zoloft killed our daughter. We are here because we believe the system we have in place is flawed. It is clear that the FDA is a political entity and its leadership has protected the economic interests of the drug industry. Under the Bush administration, the FDA has placed the interests of the drug industry over protecting the American public. . . .

Eighty-six percent of the $14 million in political contributions given by drug companies has gone to the Bush administration Republican candidates—what did Pfizer, Eli Lilly, and Glaxo-SmithKline Beecham buy? The FDA should be a jealous advocate in protecting the American people. Those in leadership positions within the FDA must be beyond reproach. FDA's chief counsel Daniel Troy has spent his career defending the drug industry. Suppressing unfavorable data may be legal, but is it ethical? If the trials don't favor a drug, the public never hears of them. Legal maneuverings have thrown out the scientific method. The drug industry must be compelled to produce all of their findings and studies. I also believe public funding of these trials is warranted. Our daughter, Julie, had been excited about college and scored 1,300 in her SATs several weeks before her death. Instead of picking out colleges with our daughter, my wife and I had to pick out a cemetery plot for her. Instead of looking forward to visiting Julie at school, we now visit her grave. The loss we have experienced is horrific. We don't want another innocent child or family to suffer this tragedy.

Part III

I am Vera Sharav and I am a resident of the Alliance for Human Research Protection. The family testimonies that you are hearing today are not anecdotes. They are corroborated by a Harvard review of children's medical charts, which found that within three months of treatment on an SSRI, 22 percent suffered drug-induced adverse psychiatric effects, and overall, 74 percent of children suffered adverse events during the course of treatment. The FDA has known for years, but failed to reveal that antidepressants consistently fail to demonstrate a benefit in children. At least 12 of 15 trials failed. The FDA has known and failed to warn physicians and the public that SSRIs increase the risk of suicide and hostility in children. FDA's 1996 Zoloft review found "7-fold greater incidence of suicidal-

DON'T RIDE WITH STRANGERS...

Chris Britt. Reproduced by permission.

ity in children treated with Zoloft than adults." The British Drug Regulatory Authority reviewed the evidence, which is not being shown in this meeting, and they determined that the risks far outweigh any benefits. They took action to protect children. When is the FDA going to take action? The FDA is foot dragging, equivocating, and tinkering with definitions while children are dying. The *San Francisco Chronicle* reports that the FDA has barred its own medical reviewer who reviewed more than 20 trials involving 4,000 children, and his findings confirmed the British finding, which is that SSRIs increase the risk of suicide.

"Media reports . . . have left the public with the impression that antidepressants cause suicidal symptoms and missed the big picture that depression causes these symptoms."

Antidepressants Do Not Increase Teen Suicide

Jim Rosack

In the following viewpoint Jim Rosack summarizes findings of a 2004 study that attributes increased suicide rates by teens on antidepressants to the fact that the drugs are prescribed for teens with the most severe disorders, who are most likely to attempt suicide. According to Rosack, the study found little difference in suicide rates for teens on selective serotonin reuptake inhibitors and other antidepressants. In addition, the study found that the suicide risk decreased the longer the patient stayed on the medication. Jim Rosack is a staff writer for Psychiatric News.

As you read, consider the following question:

1. Researchers in the study described by Rosack looked for

Jim Rosack, "New Analysis Disputes Antidepressant, Suicide Link," *Psychiatric News*, vol. 40, January 7, 2005, p. 1. Copyright © 2005 American Psychiatric Association. Reprinted with permission of the *Psychiatric News*.

any connection between what three types of incidences?

2. How did researchers determine from the medical record that a patient actually took an antidepressant medication, according to the author?

3. How did the researchers identify patient suicide attempts?

Comorbid [co-existence of more than one illness] mental illness, gender, geographic location, medication therapy, and psychotherapy are factors associated with increased rates of suicide attempts in depressed teens.

Antidepressant medications are associated with increased incidence of suicide attempts among youth because they are more likely to be prescribed to more severely ill patients—not because of the medications themselves, an innovative new analysis has determined. The analysis also found that other factors are associated with an increased risk of suicide.

The study analyzed claims data from a cohort of more than 24,000 adolescents diagnosed with major depressive disorder and tracked patients' treatment patterns and numerous factors that could influence patients to attempt suicide.

The analysis found an increased incidence of suicide attempts in adolescents treated with any antidepressant medication, not just the serotonin reuptake inhibitors. However, the association was not statistically significant, and once the researchers controlled for other potentially confounding variables, the association disappeared.

It Is Easy to Assume the Drug Made Them Do It

"People tend to look at that initial crude association [between suicide and antidepressant medication] and say, 'Well, it's higher for kids on medication, and therefore the drug made them do it,'" said Robert Valuck, Pharm. D., R.P.H., director of pharmaceutical outcomes research and an associate professor of pharmacy at the University of Colorado Health Sciences Center (UCHSC) in Denver. "But we tried to tease out as much as we could, controlling for as much as we could, and when we did, that initial relationship went away. The trend might still have been leaning [toward an association], but if anything, I think we were stepping on severity-of-illness markers."

Valuck was first author on the report, which was published in the December [2004] *CNS Drugs*. The research was investigator initiated and funded.

"We had no outside funding for this, so no one was constraining us in any way as to how we had to look at the question," Valuck noted.

"This is a very creative and methodologically rigorous analysis," commented Darrel Regier, M.D., M.P.H., executive director of the American Psychiatric Institute for Research and Education and director of APA's Division of Research. "It goes beyond the observation that suicide attempts appeared to be higher among those on antidepressants by demonstrating that these same patients happen to have more severe disorders—a major reason why they were more likely to receive medication."

Using an Incident Approach

Valuck and his team already had contracted for access to medical claims records from the PharMetrics Integrated Outcomes Database, a proprietary database of paid claims from 74 managed care plans nationwide, representing some 58 million covered individuals.

"We already had the database put together for some other depression-related research, and we had an open license to study whatever we wanted to study," Valuck explained. The team had followed the U.K. [United Kingdom] government's initial concerns regarding the use of antidepressants and suicide in teens in 2003 and began looking at a number of studies that used largely case-control approaches.

"We thought those studies had some limitations," Valuck said. "Those studies were informative, in their own way, but did not really get to the real question—which was, Do the drugs themselves increase the risk of suicide attempt?"

Rather than taking a case-control approach to the question, Valuck's group decided to use an incidence approach to look for any association between diagnosis, subsequent treatment patterns, and suicide attempt.

Propensity Analysis of Treatment and Prescriptions Filled

The group knew they would have to adjust for the lack of random assignment of the patients they were studying and the resulting potential bias. To address that inherent bias, the team created propensity or likelihood scores for each of the 24,119 adolescents identified in the database who had an index ICD-9 or -10 diagnosis of major depressive disorder or a prescription for antidepressant medication (or both) between January 1997 and March 2003. The availability of follow-up data ranged from at least six months to as long as six years, three months. Guidelines from the Centers for Disease Control and Prevention were used to identify individuals with a claim for a suicide attempt.

"We determined that, once diagnosed, each individual had a certain likelihood or not for being treated with an antidepressant. If a person was prescribed a drug, he or she had a certain likelihood for being prescribed a specific class of medication—an SSRI, a tricyclic, or multiple medications," Valuck explained.

"The use of propensity analysis is quite sophisticated and state of the art for this kind of dataset," noted Peter Jensen, M.D., the Ruane Professor of Child Psychiatry and director of

Looking at the Evidence

Evidence that antidepressants are not harmful for children include:

No suicides were reported in 25 studies of more than 4,000 children taking the pills. . . .

A 2003 World Health Organization study found that the teen suicide rate dropped in 15 nations by 33% in the past 15 years, coinciding with the widespread use of the antidepressants. In the USA, the suicide rate among adolescents dropped 25% during the past decade, the Centers for Disease Control and Prevention reported.

"Tragic teen suicides inspire idea that invites more,"
USA Today, *June 20, 2004.*

the Center for the Advancement of Children's Mental Health at Columbia University and the New York State Psychiatric Institute.

Antidepressant treatment was coded only if there was a claim for a prescription filled within 30 days of the index diagnosis. Cases for which no antidepressant claims were found at any time after diagnosis served as the control group. Cases with claims for prescriptions filled more than 30 days after the index diagnosis were excluded.

Duration of Treatment

The researchers also tracked separate measures of duration of medication therapy and patient compliance with therapy. Compliance was measured using a medication-possession ratio, equal to the total days of medication supplied divided by the time elapsed between the initial prescription and subsequent refills.

Of the 24,119 adolescents identified with an index diagnosis of major depression, 17,313 (71.8 percent) had no antidepressant prescription filled within six months of their diagnosis.

"We thought we'd see very much the opposite," Anne Libby, Ph.D., an assistant professor of psychiatry at UCHSC, noted. "The data suggest the possibility of undertreatment in this cohort."

Of those on medication, the majority were on SSRIs, followed by multiple antidepressants, "other" antidepressants, and tricyclics.

Tracking Suicide Attempts

"It's important to note," Valuck pointed out, "that this is not ideation, it's not contemplation. And it is not a measure of completion. These are events coded as suicide attempts." The majority of these events were coded in emergency rooms. Strikingly, rates of suicide attempt did not significantly differ between those on SSRIs, tricyclics, other, or multiple antidepressants. Particularly interesting, Valuck said, "was the association of suicide attempt with duration of medication therapy."

> "[Suicide risk] was elevated during that initial short period, then the longer an individual stayed on medication, the lower the risk became, and it actually became, statistically significantly, a protective effect when you got out to the guideline-based marker of 180 days."

Even after adjusting the dataset with the individually calculated propensity scores, several variables increased an adolescent's likelihood to attempt suicide. Most notably, adolescents who had a comorbid diagnosis of schizophrenia had a 3.5 higher risk of attempting suicide; having any other psychiatric disorder, including substance abuse, doubled the risk.

Taking an SSRI increased the risk of attempting suicide by 59 percent, and taking multiple antidepressant medications raised the risk 43 percent; however, neither was statistically significant. Intriguingly, the presence of a claim for at least one psychotherapy session raised the risk by a statistically significant 36 percent.

Differences by Region of the Country

Echoing earlier studies, the study found that, compared with adolescents living in the Eastern United States, adolescents living in the West were 2.7 times more likely to attempt suicide, while those in the Midwest were just over two times more likely.

Added Libby, "Simply put, those who were more severely ill were the ones who were most likely to attempt suicide. And they were the ones who were more likely to be on medication—or psychotherapy for that matter."

Thus, Valuck summed up, if people believe that the medications themselves cause suicide, then logic dictates that "we should be out there advocating for pulling the licenses of all those therapists."

Finding the Bottom Line

"We know that this is a very complicated issue, and there's lots of emotion along with political and financial influences," said Libby. "We wanted to go after a question like this because policy is being driven by it—but policy should never be based on one study or one point of view. We simply sought to contribute to the debate and provide whatever evidence we could to help narrow the focus."

Valuck and his team have submitted grant applications to look at the data in more detail. "It would be very interesting to look at to what extent provider type mattered, or what insurance plan type, copayment type, and so on mattered," he said, "and how each of those affect a youth's ability to initiate treatment and then stay in treatment."

The team has also submitted research proposals to track the effects of the black-box warnings and whether and how the warnings are changing treatment patterns and outcomes in adolescent depression.

"It's a critical issue," said Valuck. If the drugs' use in youth is restricted unnecessarily, "we could end up inducing problems over the long run."

APA's Regier concluded, "This type of analysis is much more compelling than the FDA's [Food & Drug Administration] analysis of self-reported suicidal ideation or attempts, which ignored the more systematic assessment data that showed a reduction of symptoms with treatment. Media reports of the FDA hearings have left the public with the impression that antidepressants cause suicidal symptoms and missed the big picture that depression causes these symptoms, as well as the finding, as supported by this study, that these medications need to be part of a careful treatment and monitoring plan that will reduce the overall risk of suicide."

"*Safe storage practices . . . were shown to be protective for unintentional firearm shootings and suicide attempts among adolescents.*"

Safe Gun Storage Practices Reduce the Risk of Teen Suicide

David C. Grossman et al.

Seventy-five percent of guns used in teen suicides are found in the home, claims David C. Grossman and his colleagues in the following viewpoint. In this excerpt from their study of the link between teen suicide, unintentional firearm injuries, and gun storage practices, the researchers found that keeping unloaded guns stored in a locked place separate from ammunition protects teens from suicide and accidental shootings. Based on their findings, the researchers argue in favor of safe gun storage policies. Grossman is with the Department of Preventive Care, Group Health Cooperative, in Seattle, Washington.

As you read, consider the following questions:

1. According to the authors, why are household firearms an important public health issue?

2. What do the study's authors claim are some of the differences between the storage practices of case and control guns?

3. What impact did the purpose of gun ownership have on the authors' findings?

The presence of a household firearm is associated with an increased risk of suicide among adults and adolescents. In a study of suicide attempters and completers, investigators found that 75% of the guns were stored in the residence of the victim, friend, or relative. The public health importance of household firearms is a function both of the relative risk of exposure and the prevalence of firearms in the environment of children and adolescents. [M.A.] Schuster, [T.M. Franke, A.M. Bastian, S. Sor and N. Halfon] estimated from the National Health Interview Survey that 35% of homes in the United States with children younger than 18 years reported owning at least 1 firearm, and that 43% of these homes had at least 1 unlocked firearm. Reports from other surveys have derived similar estimates of the fraction of the population at risk from unlocked household firearms.

A Need for Research

Unloading and locking all guns and ammunition in the home can potentially reduce access to guns by youth. The policy issue of safe storage of firearms, both in legislative and clinical approaches, has received much attention in the medical and public health communities over the past decade. Existing evidence supporting this approach to the prevention of firearm injuries among youth is largely derived from ecological studies of the effects of laws requiring parents to securely store firearms. Securely storing guns is perhaps a more plausible strategy for unintentional gun injuries among toddlers and young children, but the plausibility of this strategy to reduce youth suicide is less clear. A high level of intent to harm oneself may lead an actively suicidal youth to defeat gunlocks and safes.

To date, only a few studies have indirectly addressed if secure firearm storage is an effective preventive measure for either firearm suicides or unintentional firearm injuries, but few have had sufficient statistical power to detect this association. The purpose of this study was to measure the association of household firearm storage practices and the risk of unintentional and self-inflicted firearm injuries associated with child or adolescent access to firearms in the home.

The Study Design and Case Selection

This study used a case-control design, and the key exposure was firearm storage practices of guns in households with children. . . . Controls were selected from households having both firearms and exposure to children and were identified by random-digit dial telephone surveys.

A case firearm was identified by involvement in an incident in which a child or adolescent younger than 20 years gained access to a household firearm and shot himself/herself or another individual. Only suicide attempts and unintentional firearm injuries, both fatal and nonfatal, were included. . . .

Control firearms were identified from randomly selected households in the same counties from which cases were identified. A control was eligible if there was a firearm stored in or around the house (eg, in the garage, car, or attached storage area) on the date of the matched gun's shooting incident and if there was at least 1 child living or visiting the home at least 2 or more days per year under adult supervision. . . .

Examining the Results

Of the 106 shooting incidents included in the study, there were 82 suicide attempts (95% fatal) and 24 unintentional injuries (50% fatal).

Respondents from households with case and control firearms were generally similar with regard to sex, race, and whether they were homeowners or living in single-family homes. Respondents from households with case firearms were somewhat less likely to be married, a college graduate, or to have a household income of at least $70,000. They also had fewer children younger than 20 years living in the home; however, the number of children living or visiting at least 2 days per year was similar in both groups.

The median number of firearms stored in homes with case firearms was 4; the median for homes with control firearms was 3. Case firearms were more likely to be owned by a male child (21%) than were control firearms (5%).

Most of the case (49%) and control (51%) firearms were purchased new or used (25% and 20%, respectively). However, 31% of case guns were primarily for protection compared with 19% of control guns; 26% of case guns were primarily for hunting, compared with 45% of control guns. A greater proportion of case guns (39%) than control guns (27%) had been owned less than 5 years.

The Accessibility of Guns

Case guns were less likely to be stored unloaded than control guns. Similarly, case guns were less likely to be stored locked, stored separately from ammunition, or to have ammunition that was locked than were control guns. Relative to firearms that were unlocked and loaded, those stored locked and unloaded were less likely to be involved in a shooting.

The effects of accessibility of the gun and ammunition were also evaluated separately. Having only the ammunition accessible (with the reference firearm locked) was associated

Child Access Prevention Laws

Child Access Prevention (CAP) laws, or "safe storage" laws that require adults to either store loaded guns in a place that is reasonably inaccessible to children, or if they decide to leave their guns left out in the open, to use a safety device to lock the gun. If a child obtains an improperly stored, loaded gun, the adult owner is criminally liable.

Although the primary intention of CAP laws is to help prevent unintentional injury, CAP laws can also serve to reduce juvenile suicide and homicide by keeping guns out of the reach of children.

Brady Campaign to Prevent Gun Violence,
"Guns in the Home," April 2002.

with a reduced risk of a case shooting event relative to having both the gun and ammunition unlocked. Having both gun and ammunition locked was associated with an OR [odds ratio] of 0.22. Having only the gun accessible, but ammunition locked, had an OR of 0.47 for a shooting event.

The practice of locking guns with more than 1 device was not associated with any additional protective effect beyond that observed for use of a single device. The association of different extrinsic locking devices with involvement in shooting events was also assessed. Fewer case guns (32.4%) were stored at the reference date using some sort of locking device compared with control guns (57.7%). Relative to use of no device, the use of a box or safe (alone or in combination with another device) was associated with an OR of 0.26. Use of individual devices relative to nonuse of that specific device was also assessed after adjustment for use of other devices, gun loading status, and type of reference firearm. Although

ORs for use of all of the specific devices evaluated were less than 1, only the use of a lockbox/safe was associated with a statistically significant decreased OR for a firearm injury.

Although the use of different devices may vary by type of firearm, our findings related to the 4 main gun storage exposures were generally similar when analyses were stratified by whether the subject gun was a long gun or handgun. The practices of keeping the reference firearm unloaded, locked, and the ammunition locked were all associated with significantly decreased risks of a shooting event for both types of firearms. With respect to use of different devices, there were no apparent differences between devices. The ORs associated with the use of safes or lockboxes were 0.18 for long guns and 0.17 for handguns.

Regardless of whether the injury was unintentional or a suicide attempt, case guns were less likely to be stored locked or unloaded, and case ammunition was less likely to be locked.

The Purpose of Gun Ownership

Our findings remained essentially unchanged when stratified by the purpose of gun ownership, the sex of the respondent, or when the analyses excluded control guns that had never been fired. For the storage practices of keeping the gun unloaded and locked, the risk estimates were identical regardless of whether the primary purpose of the reference firearm was protection or recreation. The greatest difference observed was for the practice of keeping the gun and ammunition separate when the purpose was recreational vs when the purpose was protection.

The risk estimates for storage practices remained 0.5 or less when analyses were stratified by respondent sex with 1 exception: when the respondent included a male, the OR for keeping ammunition locked was 0.60. When firearms that had never been discharged were excluded, the greatest change occurred for the practice of keeping the gun and ammunition separate. Finally, of the households where case guns were stored, 23 respondents reported that a child was the primary owner of the gun. Because parental supervision of gun use may not be as complete in these instances, we also performed subanalyses restricted to only guns owned by adults. This restriction had no appreciable effect on the direction or magnitude of these findings, with the greatest change occurring for the practice of storing the gun and ammunition separately. All of these subanalyses, however, were limited by small numbers.

Safe Storage Practices

Safe storage practices, including keeping firearms stored unloaded, in a locked place, separate from ammunition, and/or secured with an extrinsic safety device, were shown to be protective for unintentional firearm shootings and suicide attempts among adolescents and children. The 4 specific practices of keeping a gun locked, unloaded, and storing ammunition locked and in a separate location were each associated with a protective effect and suggest feasible strategies to reduce these types of injuries in homes with children and adolescents where guns are stored. These findings appear to be consistent for both long guns and handguns, as well as for suicides and unintentional firearm injuries. . . .

The Limitations

There are a number of limitations to our study. Our findings may not be generalizable to firearm injuries resulting from homicides and criminal assaults with firearms and may not be generalizable to geographic regions not included in the study. Our study may also not be generalizable to adults or to adolescents living outside of the supervision of their parent. Our narrowly framed case definition only encompassed situations in which a supervising adult lived in the same household where the gun was stored and was aware of the presence of a gun in the household. We were unable to validate the storage status of the reference firearm; however, none of the states involved in the study had laws mandating secure storage and we found respondents rarely refused or were hesitant to disclose the storage status of guns. Furthermore, the findings of storage practices among our control households were similar to those reported in other studies of homes with children.

Recall bias is a potential threat to the validity of studies retrospectively collecting exposure data. Although we used photographs to aid identification of locking devices and few respondents appeared to have difficulty recalling this information, it is possible that memory of past storage practices may have been less accurate. When evaluated separately by whether respondents were interviewed within 1 year, or longer than 1 year from the reference date, risk estimates for storage practices were less than or equal to 0.5 with 1 exception: storing the gun separately from ammunition among those interviewed within 1 year of the reference date. . . .

In summary, storing household guns as locked, unloaded, or separate from the ammunition is associated with significant reductions in the risk of unintentional and self-inflicted firearm injuries and deaths among adolescents and children. Programs and policies designed to reduce accessibility of guns to youth, by keeping household guns locked and unloaded, deserve further attention as 1 avenue toward the prevention of firearm injuries in this population.

| "*[Common Sense about Kids and Guns] was promoting 'safe firearms storage' . . . but if they hadn't played with the numbers, they wouldn't have been able to promote their agenda.*"

Safe Gun Storage Practices Are Unnecessary

Joseph P. Tartaro

Antigun activists distort statistics about teen gun deaths to support their safe gun storage agenda, maintains Joseph P. Tartaro in the following viewpoint. Since the actual number of children killed by gun accidents or suicides is in the single digits, he claims, activists use percentages to make slight increases appear significant. Their goal is not only to promote unnecessary safe gun storage laws but to remove all guns from homes and prevent those who do not have guns from getting them, he argues. Tartaro is executive editor of Gun Week.

As you read, consider the following questions:

1. According to Tartaro, what do recent government and

National Safety Council reports reveal concerning homicides, suicides, and accidents involving firearms?

2. In the author's view, what is the job of the antigun think tanks?

3. What did *Reuters* conclude about the study of guns in the home of depressed teens?

Whenever the anti-gunners cook up a stew of numbers to support further restrictions on the lawful ownership of firearms, the media is always ready to serve that dish to an unsuspecting public.

Sometimes percentages are used when the real numbers don't count.

Sometimes the generic term "guns" is used when the numbers won't support an initiative against handguns.

These anti-gun stews have little basis in reality when it comes to public policy issues. They are intentionally concocted to support a pre-conceived agenda. And they are published in journals that cover the credentials of the so-called think tanks and policy analysts who confected them.

One of the latest of these was gobbled up by the news media and regurgitated under the headline, "Study Finds Gun Accidents, Suicides on Increase among Children."

Misleading Headlines

The headline seems to run contra to government and National Safety Council reports about homicides, suicides and accidents involving firearms which have been published in recent years. The numbers have been going down steadily, with the smallest reduction in suicides. In fact, the latest government figures indicate that there are substantially more suicides than homicides involving firearms. And the National Safety Council shows that the number of fatal firearms accidents—for children as well as the overall population—has dropped to the lowest level since such records were first published beginning near the start of the 1900s.

"Though overall firearm deaths are down nationwide, an analysis of gun accidents and suicides among kids finds that within certain age groups there were startling increases," the report on the study began.

"The greatest increases were among 5- to 9-year-olds, where the number of accidental firearm deaths increased 21% and among 10–14-year-olds, where there was a 21% increase in the number of firearm suicides.

"These findings were reported by Victoria Reggie Kennedy, president of the non-political gun safety and gun violence prevention organization Common Sense about Kids and Guns, on the one-year anniversary of the group's founding," the story continued. (Mrs. Kennedy is the wife of Sen. Edward Kennedy (D-MA).)

The "Common Sense" group is one of many such advocacy groups funded by grants from anti-gun foundations that hope to direct public policy by claiming to be "non-political" while masking their real agenda. Another such group was formed in Boulder, CO, in October [2000].

"Common Sense highlighted national mortality statistics from the Center for Disease Control's (CDC) National Center for Health Statistics that showed how overall firearm deaths for children and teens (0–19) were down 10% in 1998, but non-homicide firearm deaths (i.e., accidents and suicides) only declined 4% from 1997 to 1998 (from 1,643 to 1,577)," the report continued.

"Common Sense," which focuses on parental responsibility for preventing kids' unsupervised access to guns, pointed out that in non-homicide categories, especially among younger kids, there were actually increases.

The Numbers Paint a Different Picture

But when you look past the percentages at the real numbers, a different picture emerges.

The media reports said: "The study found that:

- "—For kids under 15, non-homicide firearm deaths increased 4% (from 283 to 295)."

- "—Among 5–9-year-olds, accidental firearm deaths increased 21% (28 to 34)."

- "—Among 10–14-year-olds, firearm suicides increased 21% (126 to 153)."

When you go back and look at the real numbers, you see that for kids under 15, non-homicide firearms deaths in the period increased by a total of 8 nationwide.

And among children between 5 and 9 years old, there was an actual increase of 6 in the total of accidental firearms deaths.

Long ago in journalism school, we were instructed to never say "only" in connection with any number of deaths. But in this case, "only" is relevant because it provides a more realistic evaluation of what "Common Sense" really has to say. Using such numbers to produce scary percentages is statistical tom-foolery. When the numbers themselves don't add up, and there is no significant trend, resort to percentages.

This is essentially the kind of reality that John Lott, senior researcher at Yale University, used to debunk the firearms accident claims of Gov. Parris Glendening in Maryland. The governor was promoting his trigger lock and "smart gun" legislation with inflated claims.

When Lott checked the numbers, he found that there had been two such incidents in the period the governor cited.

The Safe-Storage Agenda

The report on the "Common Sense" study eventually made it clear that the organization was promoting "safe firearms storage"—that is gun locks and "smart guns." But if they hadn't played with the numbers, they wouldn't have been able to promote their agenda at all. They needed a hook for their PR and percentages gave them one. How many headlines would they have gotten if they had started by saying that 8 or 6 more children in those age groups had been killed accidentally during their study period?

The job of the anti-gun think tanks is to come up with headlines that will change public opinion. If they have to fudge the numbers, they will do so.

While the first story was making headlines, another by *Reuters* "Health" news service, claimed that guns remain in homes of depressed teens. This so-called study is linked to the relatively new policy of some health professionals to intervene in the family affairs of patients with guns.

"Even after being told by a health professional that keeping a gun at home may increase the likelihood that a depressed child will attempt suicide, most parents of depressed teens do not remove firearms from their homes, according to a new study," *Reuters* said.

"The high proportion of families who, after receiving information, continued to keep a gun in the house is concerning, given the apparent risk for suicide conveyed by a gun in the home and the 30-fold increased risk for suicide conveyed by adolescent depression," Dr. David A. Brent and colleagues at the University of Pittsburgh in Pennsylvania wrote in the October [2000] issue of *The Journal of the American Academy of Child and Adolescent Psychiatry.*

"Based on research indicating that depressed teens who live in homes where a gun is present are more likely to attempt suicide than those living in firearm-free homes," Brent and his colleagues began asking parents of teens treated for depression in an outpatient clinic whether they had a gun at home. If the family did have a gun at home, parents were counseled on the suicide risks of keeping a gun at home and advised to remove the gun from the house. If there was not a gun in the home, however, the parents and patients were not counseled on the dangers of keeping a gun at home.

Promoting Gun-Free Homes

"Most parents did not heed the advice about making their homes gun-free zones," the researchers report. During a child's treatment and up to 2 years later, guns were removed from only one-fourth to one-third of the houses that had firearms.

"And some homes that were previously gun-free had firearms present at the end of the study. In fact, about one out of every six such households obtained a gun by the end of the 2-year follow-up period," the report claimed.

At this point, you might have guessed what the recommendation for future action would be, but here is what *Reuters* reported was the conclusion:

"The results of the study show that doctors and other health professionals need to do more to make parents of depressed teens aware of the risks of having a gun at home, including discussing the issue with families who do not have firearms to ensure that their homes remain gun-free, according to the researchers."

There you have it. These researchers don't want to merely remove guns, they also want to be sure the families that don't already have firearms don't become gunowners.

"Homosexuality is an important risk factor for adolescent suicide."

Homosexuality Is a Risk Factor in Teen Suicide

Robert Li Kitts

The psychological and social stress associated with being gay increases the risk of suicide among gay teens, maintains Robert Li Kitts in the following viewpoint. Society continues to disapprove of homosexuality, which adds to the stress experienced by gay teens, he argues. Some gay teens are rejected by family and friends, Kitts claims, leaving them with fewer resources to help them solve problems and cope with stress. Suicide risk factors such as depression, substance abuse, and homelessness are also more common among gay teens, he asserts. Kitts is a psychiatry resident at Oregon Health and Science University.

As you read, consider the following questions:

1. In Kitts's opinion, why do physicians not discuss their patients' sexual history?
2. What have several studies revealed about gay and lesbian

Robert Li Kitts, "Gay Adolescents and Suicide: Understanding the Association," *Adolescence*, vol. 40, Fall 2005, pp. 621–628. Copyright © 2005 Libra Publishers, Inc. Reproduced by permission.

adolescents and violence?

3. According to the author, what are some of the negative family outcomes of gay teens who come out?

A 16-year-old male with depression has committed suicide. He had been seeing a physician who placed him on an anti-depressant three weeks ago. His family, friends, and physician knew of his depression, but did not know why he was depressed or why he committed suicide. Was he hiding an unbearable secret? Homosexuality was never brought up. His parents could not conceive of the idea and it was not accepted by their religion. His male friends would always talk about girls with him, and occasionally made gay jokes, but he never seemed to mind. His physician assumed he was heterosexual because he had a girlfriend in the past. In actuality, he was confused, scared, and alone. He thought he liked girls, but he had been feeling more attracted to boys. He could not control these feelings despite the fear that his parents would disown him and his friends would turn on him. He had no one to talk to and was afraid his physician might be homophobic and reveal his feelings to his mother, who was always sitting right outside the office. Fortunately, this is a fictional case, but how many suicides resemble this?

A Lack of Coping Strategies

Approximately one million adolescents attempt suicide per year. Every 90 minutes one adolescent commits suicide, making it the third leading cause of death among ten- to 19-year-olds. To explain the high suicide rate. [H.] Kaplan and [B.] Sadock (2003) state, "Universal features in suicidal adolescents are the inability to synthesize solutions to problems and the lack of coping strategies to deal with immediate stressors. Therefore, a narrow view of the options available to deal with recurrent family discord, rejection, or failure contributes to a decision to commit suicide." For gay adolescents this reasoning is far more pronounced. The process of realizing that one is gay and having to accept it is not just an immediate stressor and can actually narrow one's options further by taking away coping resources, such as friends and family. Gay adolescents who "come out" (disclose their sexuality) may experience great family discord, rejection, and even failure from the disappointment they elicit. It would make sense to conclude that homosexuality is an important risk factor for adolescent suicide. However, many physicians disagree and textbooks fail to adequately emphasize this point. This reflects the need to understand the increased risk of suicide among gay adolescents. . . .

Why Is Sexual History Seldom Discussed?

[M.] Nusbaum and [C.] Hamilton (2002) reported a study in which only 35% of primary healthcare physicians reported that they often (75% of the time) or always take a sexual history. Two of their explanations for the low percentage were embarrassment and the belief that it is irrelevant to the chief complaint. Sex is still an uncomfortable and embarrassing subject for many people, even for physicians. As a result, the tendency is to avoid it. When interviewing an adolescent who is depressed or suicidal how often is sexuality questioned? And if it is brought up, is it discussed and in how much detail? How does the adolescent feel about answering such questions, especially if he/she does not know how gay-friendly the physician is. Sexuality may seem irrelevant to the physician who is seeing an adolescent whose chief complaint is depression or suicidal ideation—and therefore ignores the subject.

There is still a stigma attached to being openly gay even in the medical field. During a small conference on gay issues at my former medical university, one of the deans referred to the medical environment as not being the most open-minded and cautioned students to be careful about revealing their sexuality. For some people, not just gays, there is the fear that if one brings up a gay issue or gives a lecture on it, one will be assumed to be gay, especially if one is not married. Unless it is my "gay paranoia," I would not be surprised if readers of this article assumed I was gay. This was a risk I was hesitant to take. Unfortunately, it is a risk that some physicians are not willing to take out of fear of jeopardizing their careers. This fear hinders important gay issues from being discussed in the mainstream. Goldfried (2001) stated that despite the growing literature on gay issues, mainstream psychology has tended to ignore much of the work that has been done in this area. Thus, important issues, such as suicide among gay adolescents, remain invisible not only to mainstream psychology, but to mainstream healthcare.

During a lecture at the same university noted, a public health physician asked, "What are some risk factors for adolescent suicide?" After waiting for everyone else's response, I finally said, "homosexuality." The physician was unsure about this answer and turned to the psychiatrist who currently held a fellowship in child and adolescent psychiatry. To my surprise, he stated, "I do not think so."

An Increased Risk

Being a gay adolescent is a significant risk factor for suicidal thoughts and attempts. More than 15 different studies conducted within the last 20 years have consistently showed significantly higher rates of suicide attempts, in the range of 20 to 40%, among gay adolescents. [S.] Russell and [K.] Joyner (2001) were the first to use nationally representative data to support this association. In a study involving over 6,000 adolescent girls and over 5,000 adolescent boys, they concluded that adolescents with a same-sex orientation were more than twice as likely to attempt suicide.

How many suicides occur without learning whether the person was gay? People commit suicide leaving family and friends asking, "Why?" Could it be because of a secret they

Statistics on Teen Suicide

Suicide is the eighth leading cause of death in America and is skyrocketing amongst our youth. For young people ages 15–24, suicide is the third leading cause of death. As staggering as these numbers may appear, it is widely believed that suicide amongst gay, lesbian and bisexual youth is even more profound—According to Paul Gibson, "gay and lesbian youth have a two to three fold risk of suicide" compared to heterosexual youth. In a recent study, 5 out of every 8 suicide attempters were gay or bisexual—or put another way, gay and bisexual youth are 13.6 times more likely to have attempted suicide than their heterosexual counterparts.

Suicide amongst gay, lesbian and bisexual youth is a serious problem. As members of a hated, harassed and rejected group, these youth experience a sense of being different and isolated in the world, and they are at high risk for severe depression and suicide.

Shaun Bourget, GayHealth.com. 09/05/00.
www.AlterHeros.com.

could not bear revealing—such as being gay? One study involving 350 gay adolescents between the ages of 14 and 21 reported that 54% made their first suicide attempt before coming out to others, 27% made the attempt during the same year they came out, and 19% made the attempt after coming out.

Since being a gay adolescent is a risk factor for suicide, it needs to be addressed within the medical community. Physicians can help by raising the issue when appropriate on rounds, in case conferences, or during lectures. Addressing the issue of sexuality with adolescents can be made easier and more effective if the physician understands why it is so unbearable for some adolescents to reveal their sexuality or to live with being gay.

Understanding the Association

Being gay in-and-of-itself is not the cause of the increase in suicide. The increased risk comes from the psychosocial distress associated with being gay. Six studies reported by [G.] Remafedi (1999) found that suicide attempts were significantly associated with psychosocial stressors, including gender nonconformity, early awareness of being gay, victimization, lack of support, school dropout, family problems, acquaintances' suicide attempts, homelessness, substance abuse, and other psychiatric disorders. Some of these stressors are also experienced by heterosexual adolescents, but they have been shown to be more prevalent among gay adolescents. In Russell and Joyner's (2001) study using national data, adolescents who reported same-sexual orientation also reported significantly more substance abuse, depression, acquaintances' suicide attempts, and victimization. Thus, physicians can be more helpful in improving gay adolescents' quality of life by understanding their psychosocial stress load and its impact on suicide risk.

By noting the changes taking place in the media and the law, it is apparent that being gay is somewhat more accepted and tolerated by today's society. However, gays are still being discriminated against and victimized. [S.] Russell [B. Franz, and A. Driscoll] (2001) reported a study involving 500 gay and lesbian adolescents in which it was found that 41% had experienced violence, and 46% of that violence was reported as being related to being gay. In a study by [D.] Bontempo and [A.] D'Augelli involving over 9,000 9th through 12th graders, 24% of gay/bisexual males reported at-school victimization ten or more times per year as compared with 2.7% of their heterosexual counterparts, and 10.1% of lesbian/

165

bisexual females compared with 1.1% of their female counterparts. These negative experiences can result in mood disorders, lower self-esteem, posttraumatic stress symptoms, substance abuse, and suicide.

An adolescent does not need to be directly victimized to be affected by discrimination against gays. Matthew Shephard, a University of Wyoming student, was brutally murdered in 1998 because he was gay. What impact did this devastating event have on young individuals who were beginning to realize that they too were gay and living in the same society in which the murder was praised? What messages are protestors and politicians, including our President, who are against gay marriage sending to gay adolescents? How does living in a society where people can be rejected, disapproved of, or hated for their sexuality affect a gay adolescent's self-esteem or identity development? (Nelson, 1997).

Rejection by Friends and Family

Further, what may be even worse than being hated by society because of one's sexuality is being rejected, humiliated, and victimized by one's own family or peers. Gay adolescents have a much greater incidence of being thrown out of or opting to leave their homes. In a study involving 194 gay adolescents between the ages of 14 and 21, D'Augelli et al. (1998) reported that 26% of fathers, 10% of mothers, and 15% of siblings rejected their gay children when they came out. [M.] Goldfried (2001) reported that one out of every three were verbally abused by family members, one out of ten were physically assaulted by a family member, and one out of four had experienced physical abuse at school. The fear of experiencing such outcomes can be a tremendous stressor. How does a gay, closeted child feel when living with parents who adamantly reject gay marriage? Only 10 to 14% of gay adolescents who had not come out to their parents predicted parental acceptance. How do these negative outcomes or fear of such negative outcomes also affect an adolescent's self-esteem or identity development? [J.] Nelson (1974) points out that gay adolescents who report a history of a suicide attempt score significantly lower on scales of family support, self-perception and self-esteem, and extra-familial social support when compared to similar adolescents without a reported history of suicidal ideation or suicide attempts.

Physicians can help by strengthening the support structure needed by some gay adolescents. Physicians should have information about such resources as PFLAG (Parents, Family, and Friends of Lesbians and Gays) and community gay centers so that they can refer patients and their families for assistance. National associations such as the Gay and Lesbian Medical Association, Association of Gay and Lesbian Psychiatrists, and the Lesbian and Gay Child and Adolescent Psychiatric Association have openly gay physicians who welcome referrals. . . .

A gay adolescent may have to deal with many of the problems that have been discussed along with the typical stressors that come with being an adolescent. Thus, it should be no surprise that there is an increase in suicide risk for this population. Hopefully, a better understanding of the psychosocial issues associated with being gay will enable physicians to be more comfortable with their gay adolescent patients' problems, foster more open relationships, help them feel more accepted, and ultimately, help prevent adolescent suicide.

| "Sexual orientation per se is not a risk factor for [adolescent] suicide attempts."

Homosexuality Is Not a Risk Factor in Teen Suicide

Ritch C. Savin-Williams and Geoffrey L. Ream

In the following viewpoint, Ritch C. Savin-Williams and Geoffrey L. Ream contest previous research that identified homosexuality as a risk factor for teen suicide. Life stressors such as substance abuse and social isolation—not sexual orientation per se—lead to suicide attempts, they assert. According to the authors, the rate of suicide among all gay teens is indistinguishable from the suicide rate among heterosexual teens. Savin-Williams is professor of human development at Cornell University. In May 2005 Ream received his PhD in developmental psychology from Cornell.

As you read, consider the following questions:

1. What was the nature of the gay youth population sampled in the investigation that Savin-Williams and Ream dispute?

Ritch C. Savin-Williams and Geoffrey L. Ream, "Suicide Attempts Among Sexual Minority Male Youth," *Journal of Clinical Child and Adolescent Psychology*, vol. 32, 2003, pp. 509–522. Copyright © 2003 by Lawrence Erlbaum Associates, Inc. All rights reserved. Reproduced by permission.

2. How were participants in the authors' study selected?

3. In the authors' opinion, what is it more critical to explore in predicting whether youth report a suicide attempt?

The prevalence and causes of suicidality have been major concerns of adolescent psychologists during the last half-century. Although the rate of suicide among adolescents is no higher than among adults, adolescent suicide has received considerably greater attention because the tragic "waste" of young lives has captured the imaginations of researchers, educators, and mental health professionals. National data indicate that during the preceding 12 months, 14% of male and 25% of female high school students "seriously considered attempting suicide." 11% and 18% (boys and girls, respectively) had made a "specific plan to attempt suicide," 6% and 11% (boys and girls, respectively) "had attempted suicide," and 2% and 3% (boys and girls, respectively) had made a suicide attempt that resulted in "an injury, poisoning, or overdose that had to be treated by a doctor or nurse." Endeavoring to reduce the death toll, researchers have probed whether particular youth are at increased risk for suicide by investigating individual characteristics (e.g., impulsivity, sexual orientation), family variables (e.g., divorce, family climate), peer reactions (e.g., bullying, peer rejection), and community stressors (e.g., poverty, discrimination).

One individual-level characteristic that has received substantial attention during the last two decades is a gay, lesbian, or bisexual identification. Prevalence rates of suicide attempts among such youth average 30% to 40% and have been generally attributed to environmental reactions to their same-sex sexuality. The overwhelming consensus is that gay youth are highly and disproportionately at risk for attempting suicide. This led [G. Remafedi] to declare. "The evidence is sufficiently compelling to warrant the education of mental health professionals as well as the development of preventive interventions for GLB youth. It is time to put the controversy [whether gay youth are at risk for suicide] aside and be about the business of saving lives." In their review, [J.S.] McDaniel and [D. Purcell, and A.R. D'Angelli] (2001) asserted, "It is reasonable to conclude that the difference in suicide attempts is well established."

Controversial Conclusions

Controversy exists, however, based on methodological issues, including the unrepresentative nature of the gay youth population sampled. Many investigations were conducted, by design, with youth most likely to be suffering physically, psychologically, and socially—those attending urban-based support groups or willing to identify themselves as gay on high school questionnaires [P.] Muehrer (1995) warned. "Conclusions about gay and lesbian youth in the general population may not be drawn from nonrepresentative settings such as crisis centers, runaway shelters, or support groups, where self-referred youth in distress are found."

In addition, only a few empirical studies have systematically addressed whether factors that predict suicide attempts among gay youth are the same ones that predict suicidality among heterosexual youth. That is, are gay youth at increased risk because of unique factors associated with their sexual orientation (e.g., disclosure to family, negative societal attitudes toward homosexuality, antigay victimization) or because of elevated levels of factors associated with suicide in all youth (e.g., depression, low self-esteem, substance abuse)? . . .

The Problem with Sexual Minority Research

In this investigation, we address [L.M.] Diamond's "four problems" [the excerpts selected explore the first three] associated with research on sexual minorities and apply them toward an analysis of data on sexual-minority youth suicidality. First, Diamond notes that research often confuses precepts about who belongs in various sexual categories. To the extent that it is possible through secondary analysis of datasets that were not explicitly collected for this purpose, we define a same-sex sexual orientation, sexual behavior, and self–identification as gay, lesbian, or bisexual and investigate whether they are differentially linked with suicidality.

Second, Diamond argues that research often fails to document whether features of sexual orientation per se matter in predicting distinct or salient outcomes independent of sexual orientation. We test this by investigating whether sexual orientation, as operationalized by [A.C.] Kinsey, [W.B.] Pomeroy, and [C.E.] Martin's (1948) continuum of same-sex to opposite-sex attractions, uniquely explains a significant amount of variance in the prevalence and predictors of suicide attempts.

Third, Diamond points out that research too often assumes that sexual-minority populations are monolithic, thereby neglecting diversity and within-group variations. We address this concern by assessing whether youth who attend an urban support group vary from those who do not in terms of differential experiences of and vulnerability to stress. . . .

We focus exclusively on male youth because the available datasets did not contain sufficient number of young women for analysis.

The Participants

Youth who contributed to the Detroit dataset were recruited in collaboration with Katherine Wright, a pediatrician at Children's Hospital of Michigan in Detroit. A health-based survey was administered to youth attending Affirmations, a gay support group. At the initial visit in 1994, 29 of 31 male youth in attendance agreed to participate. All additional male youth present at a 10-month follow-up agreed to participate.

These 51 young men (age range 14 to 23 years) constituted the sample. . . .

Although drawbacks exist to Internet sources and techniques of data collection, such as self-selection of participants based on Internet connection, the impossibility of calculating a response rate, and the difficulty of verifying response accuracy, it also offers unique accessibility to hidden populations of stigmatized youth who might be at a preidentity or predisclosure point in their sexual development and thus might not otherwise participate in "gay research."

The 681 participants were young men between the ages of 13 and 25 years who responded to a World Wide Web questionnaire, the OutProud/Oasis Internet Survey of Queer and Questioning Youth, between September 1 and October 31, 2000. The original sample contained 1,016 male youth from 73 countries. . . .

Using two datasets based on the incidence and associations of suicide attempts among same-sex attracted youth, these findings provided initial answers to Diamond's four questions for research on sexual minorities. As such, it offers a model of how research on sexual minorities can become more sophisticated and compelling.

Is It Orientation, Behavior, or Identity?

In distinguishing sexual-minority youth reporting suicide attempts, it did not matter if youth rated themselves as being exclusively, predominantly, significantly, or incidentally attracted to other boys or if they labeled themselves as gay or not. In addition, whether youth reported sex with another boy was also not associated with suicide attempt status.

Previous investigations rarely tested whether suicidality varies by these definitions of sexual-minority status, although some have assumed that youth with same-sex attractions who had not adopted a label were the most troubled and hence would be at greatest risk for a variety of mental health problems, including depression, anxiety, substance abuse, and suicidality. This investigation failed to support this assumption—whether a same-sex attracted youth identified as gay was not associated with suicidality status.

If the definitional issue, however, was not same-sex behavior but the context in which sex occurred, then relevance was established. An early age of first male sex, a large number of male partners, and permissive attitudes or behaviors regarding unsafe sex were related to a greater likelihood of reporting a suicide attempt. Although others have reported similar results, it is unclear what drives the relation. Given the relation of unsafe sex (which could include early and frequent sex) with other risk factors such as low self-esteem and substance abuse, it is not sex with another boy that is associated with suicide attempts but its association with risk factors.

Thus, in predicting whether youth report a suicide attempt, it is less critical as to how youth are defined in terms of their degree of same-sex attractions, behavior, or identity than to explore their associations with known risk factors, such as where the population is drawn or psychosocial and behavioral characteristics of the population. These are explored in the following.

Is Sexual Orientation per se a Risk Factor?

Most researchers deny the existence of anything inherently suicidal about a same-sex orientation. It is not same-sex attractions that cause one to be suicidal, but rather environmental reactions (victimization, discrimination, and harassment) to those who claim a gay identity that are the causative agents that lead to a stressful and difficult life for gay youth. Researchers do not agree, however, as to the direct or indirect connection between suicidality and specific environmental events. Although [S.L.] Hershberger and [A.R.] D'Augelli (1995) were unable to statistically elucidate the mechanisms by which victimization led to suicidality, "the association exists and

No Link Between Gay Teens and Suicide Has Been Proven

The discussions revolving around gay teens and suicide have been so contentious within the research community that a conference was convened [in 1994] to address the alleged link between suicide and sexual orientation. In the end, representatives of the Centers for Disease Control, the National Institute of Mental Health, the American Psychological Association, the American Academy of Suicidology, and gay and lesbian advocacy and service groups dispelled any notion of a direct or indirect link.

It simply had not been proven.

Delia M. Rios, (New Orleans) Times-Picayune, *May 17, 1998.*

should not be dismissed." Others found gay-related stressors (e.g., disclosure to parents, peer ridicule) rather than general life-events stressors or sexual orientation, explained considerable variance in suicide attempts.

Theoretically and practically, however, it is challenging to separate the two. Life stressors such as substance abuse and social isolation can be explained by both gay-related factors (use of substances to blunt the fear that friends will discover one's homosexuality) and factors independent of sexual orientation (e.g., poverty, temperament). For their part, gay youth seldom attribute the bulk of "blame" for their suicidality to their sexuality.

The link between sexual orientation and suicidality was at best weak in the OutProud survey. First, nearly 80% of participants had *never or rarely* seriously considered suicide. No one who survived to participate in the survey indicated an attempt was intended to be lethal or used means known to be successful. Most youths who reported an attempt did not want or intend to die, and 90% made sure they used nonlethal means. Given that few youth substantially placed themselves in meaningful danger, a previous assertion that some youth who *report* suicide attempts might never have attempted suicide was indirectly supported.

Comparing our data with "normative" Centers for Disease Control teenage male data and previous research on adolescent suicidality, we conclude that sexual orientation per se is not a risk factor for suicide attempts. Although a disproportionate number of gay youth may be experiencing sufficient personal conflict and distress to report a suicide attempt, because we were careful not to conflate sexual status with risk behaviors related to sexuality, sexual-minority status in and of itself does not appear to place young people at disproportionate risk for suicide attempts.

Does It Matter Where Youth Are Recruited?

To address Diamond's concern that researchers too often ignore diversity within sexual-minority populations, we compared youth who had attended a gay support group with those who had not. One of the most frequent and ardent criticisms of the empirical suicide attempt literature is exactly this point—research designs are set up to find a sexual orientation difference in suicidality because the sampled gay population is narrowly defined as those most likely to be suicidal. Indeed, in our Detroit data (the traditional study population), the support-group partition of the OutProud sample corroborated these findings. Because of the measures used, it was not possible to evaluate whether the high suicide attempt rate was artificially inflated due to the presence of false attempts (i.e., a reported attempt that did not occur)—a critical issue ignored in previous studies.

The Internet dataset allowed us a unique opportunity to assess population diversity among sexual-minority youth by including non-support group youth, who constituted the vast majority (84%) of those who responded to the survey. These youth appeared "less gay"—less likely to have sex with another boy, to be exclusively gay, to have disclosed to others, to claim a gay sexual identity, and to feel comfortable being gay. They seldom engaged in unsafe sex, were victimized for being gay, and used substances. In terms of suicidality, their prevalence rate was similar to the national average for teenage boys.

It would be nonsensical, based on these data, to argue that support groups caused youth to be suicidal. Although the variance between youth was only partially explained by these analyses, they suggest that youth who attend support groups do so for a reason—because they need support. Youth might well benefit from support groups in terms of greater self-acceptance, lower internalized homophobia, and more opportunities to meet sexual or romantic partners, but these benefits do not completely offset detriments associated with greater victimization experiences and substance use among these youth—which they likely experienced prior to attending a support group.

These findings attest to the diversity within sexual-minority populations, including differential levels of risk exposure and vulnerability. Thus, depending on the subpopulation under study, the suicide attempt rate among gay youth ranges from catastrophic levels to rates indistinguishable from heterosexual youth. . . .

Although this research focused on the suicidality of sexual-minority youth, it is critical to emphasize that the vast majority of same-sex attracted youth in the OutProud dataset rarely or never seriously considered suicide, never planned a suicide, and never attempted suicide—a point seldom emphasized in previous research. In addition, despite the fact that half of the sexual-minority youth had been victimized, few had low self-esteem, were depressed, abused substances, or would change their sexual orientation. Most had accepted their sexuality and felt good about it. Indeed, perhaps at long last we can lay to rest the suicidality controversy, moving past the moot question of whether gay youth are suicidal to address the more appropriate question of *which* youth are suicidal and how being a sexual minority informs that experience. The first step in this direction is acknowledgment that, although conventional wisdom on gay youth portends tragedy and pathos, relatively few sexual-minority male youth follow the "suffering suicidal script."

Periodical Bibliography

American Academy of
Child and Adolescent
Psychology

"Teen Suicide," www.aacap.org.

American Association
of Suicidology

"About Suicide," www.suicidology.org.

John F. Desmond

"Walker Percy and Suicide," *Modern Age*,
Winter 2005.

Diedtra Henderson

"FDA Studies Teen Suicide Link to Antidepressants," *Chicago Sun-Times*, September 14, 2004.

Willow Lawson

"Holiday Suicide Myth," *Psychology Today*,
November/December 2003.

Iris Manor, Michel
Vincent, and Sam Tyano

"The Wish to Die and the Wish to Commit
Suicide in the Adolescent: Two Different Matters?" *Adolescence*, Summer 2004.

Cheryl Miller

"The Long Goodbye: Helping Kids Cope with
Suicide," *Group*, September/October 2005.

National Center for
Injury Prevention and
Control

"Suicide: Fact Sheet," www.cdc.gov.

Philip A. Rutter and
Andrew E. Behrendt

"Adolescent Suicide Risk: Four Psychosocial
Factors," *Adolescence*, Summer 2004.

Philip A. Rutter and
Emil Soucar

"Youth Suicide Risk and Sexual Orientation,"
Adolescence, Summer 2002.

CHAPTER 4

Should Physician-Assisted Suicide Be Condoned?

Chapter Preface

On October 5, 2005, the U.S. Supreme Court heard oral arguments in *Gonzales v. Oregon*, a case that challenges the Oregon Death with Dignity Act, which legalized physician-assisted suicide in that state. Alberto Gonzales, the U.S. attorney general, contends that under the federal Controlled Substances Act (CSA), the use of a lethal drug to assist suicide is not a "legitimate medical purpose" and, therefore, is prohibited. He claims that the CSA provides for federal control of "all manufacturing, possession, and distribution of any scheduled drug." Oregon's Death with Dignity Act, however, authorizes physicians, under certain conditions, to prescribe such drugs when a terminally ill patient requests aid in dying.

Plaintiffs for Oregon argue that assisted suicide was made a legal medical practice under Oregon law when voters approved the Death with Dignity Act in 1997. The Oregon plaintiffs further contend that the CSA was intended only to allow federal regulation of "trafficking in illegal drugs, such as heroin and marijuana, and . . . diversion of legitimately produced controlled substances into illicit channels." In their view, the act has no bearing on physicians' use of drugs to help terminally ill patients die.

People on both sides of the physician-assisted suicide debate monitored the case closely. For those opposed to the practice of assisted suicide, Oregon's law sets a dangerous precedent. They worry that since the practice is legal there, other states will enact similar laws. They believe that if Oregon doctors who participate in physician-assisted suicide could be prosecuted under federal law, efforts to legalize assisted dying elsewhere would effectively end. As a result, they support the federal government's position in *Gonzales v. Oregon*. On the other hand, proponents of assisted suicide support Oregon in the case. They recognize the importance of Oregon's law in making it easier to legalize physician-assisted suicide in other states. These commentators view the government's case as an attempt to get around a law enacted by a majority of Oregon voters in order to end efforts to make assisted suicide legal elsewhere.

As this volume went to press, *Gonzales v. Oregon* was decided: The court ruled in favor of Oregon. The Supreme Court's decision likely will have an enormous impact on the movement to make physician-assisted suicide legal. The authors in this chapter contribute to the long-standing debate over physician-assisted suicide by considering whether or not assisted suicide should be condoned for any reasons.

"Assisted suicide cannot be considered a 'legitimate medical purpose' or 'treatment.'"

Physician-Assisted Suicide Violates Medical Ethics

Physicians for Compassionate Care Educational Foundation

On October 5, 2005, the U.S. Supreme Court began hearing oral arguments in Gonzales v. Oregon, *in which the U.S. attorney general sought to prohibit Oregon physicians from prescribing controlled substances to assist terminally ill patients in dying. Under Oregon's Death with Dignity Act, such acts had been legal. In the following viewpoint a physicians' organization argues that physician-assisted suicide (PAS) is incompatible with the physician's role as a healer. Physicians for Compassionate Care contends that the Oregon law endangers patients because the physician is exempt from meeting ordinary standards of care. The Physicians for Compassionate Care Educational Foundation is dedicated to preserving the traditional role of physicians to heal patients and minimize pain.*

As you read, consider the following questions:

Physicians for Compassionate Care Educational Foundation, "Amicus Brief for Physicians for Compassionate Care Educational Foundation in Support of Petioners," *Gonzales v. Oregon*, Supreme Court of the United States.

1. The Oregon Death with Dignity Act protects physicians who assist in suicides from professional discipline thus replacing traditional "standards of care" with what?

2. In the case of Michael P. Freeland cited in the brief, how long had Freeland had suicidal feelings?

3. When volunteers for Physicians for Compassionate Care Education Foundation arrived on the scene in the final weeks of Freeland's life, what pain medication was he taking?

The dispensing of drugs to assist a person in committing suicide is not a "legitimate medical purpose", nor is it "treatment" within the meaning of the Controlled Substances Act (CSA), a conclusion maintained by 49 States, the federal government, and leading associations of the medical profession.

Oregon's Death with Dignity Act does not allow for doctor-assisted suicide within the context of a "legitimate medical purpose." The Act functions by singling out a particular class of individuals and excluding them from the normal protections generally afforded medical patients. In particular, the Act exempts Oregon doctors who write deliberately lethal prescriptions from meeting the accepted standard of care, and otherwise conforming their practice to the ethical standards of the medical profession. Oregon's Death with Dignity Act is a radical departure from the long-accepted legal and ethical norms of the medical profession and puts a defined group of patients and their families beyond the protections afforded by these protocols.

Specifically, the Act disallows recourse to malpractice suits by these patients and their family members in that it exempts assisted-suicide doctors from the requirement of meeting the ordinary standards of medical care in like communities nationally, and instead holds them only to a "good faith" standard, which is something heretofore unknown in a medical-legal sense, and inapplicable to any legitimate medical treatment. [The Act] states, "No person shall be subject to civil or criminal liability or professional disciplinary action for participating in good faith compliance with [the Act]." The statute actually replaces traditional "standard of care" requirements with a "good faith" standard that is, in essence, totally subjective, and virtually impossible to evaluate within the established context of medical practice, and treats assisted-suicide as different from any legitimate medical purpose or treatment.

Oregon Law Protects Physicians

Furthermore, the Act protects physicians who facilitate suicide against any professional discipline, provided only that the physician act in "good faith". Specifically, the Act provides, "No professional organization or association, or health care provider, may subject a person to censure, discipline, suspension, loss of license, loss of privileges, loss of membership or other penalty for participating or refusing to participate in good faith compliance with [provisions of the Act]." At the same time, the American Medical Association, the American Nurses Association, and the American Psychiatric Association have all stated in a joint brief in *Washington v. Glucksberg*, that physician-assisted suicide is "fundamentally incompatible with the physician's role as healer". This statement is derived from the published ethics of the American Medical Association, Handbook of Medical Ethics, and emphasizes that assisted-suicide, as determined by the medical profession, not only falls outside the bounds of ethical medical practice, it is actually incompatible with medical practice.

Adherence to the ethical standards of the American Medical Association is also required by and for membership in the Oregon Medical Association. Oregon is the only state that has so radically departed from accepted standards so as to allow for assisted-suicide, by removing this specific procedure from the ethical requirements of the prevailing medical organizations, and which otherwise apply to all other legitimate medical treatments within its borders. These facts further demonstrate the reasonableness of the Attorney General's conclusion based on the Office of Legal Counsel memorandum, dated June 27, 2001, that assisted suicide cannot be considered a "legitimate medical purpose" or "treatment."

An Example of a Patient Treated Improperly

The case of Michael P. Freeland poignantly demonstrates how Oregon's radical deviation from the long-accepted legal and ethical norms has resulted in the abuse of federally controlled substances to the detriment of innocent and vulnerable patients. This case is the only case involving a patient who was prescribed assisted-suicide drugs in Oregon that is based on an actual outside examination of medical records, court documents, and patient and family interviews. The official Oregon reports, which have been so roundly criticized as more protective of the Oregon Death with Dignity Act than of the vulnerable patients derives almost all of its information from the assisted-suicide doctors themselves.

Mr. Freeland, an Oregon resident, developed lung cancer in his early sixties. Suicidal feelings had haunted him since he was twenty-one after his mother had died from a self-inflicted gunshot wound. Freeland actually attempted suicide shortly after his mother's death and was treated for depression in a psychiatric hospital. Still preoccupied with suicide, he made at least two additional suicide attempts. On each occasion, his suicidal despair was treated according to the generally accepted standards of medical care: he was deprived access to lethal means; he was protected until his suicidal impulses

185

A DISPOSABLE SOCIETY

Michael Ramirez. Reproduced by permission.

abated; and he was treated for depression and any other factors contributing to his despair.

With the treatment, Mr. Freeland did reasonably well until, when in his sixties, he was officially categorized as "terminally ill" in Oregon. Not surprisingly, his physician and a consultant chosen by that doctor opined that Freeland had a "terminal cancer", as defined by the Act, because, in their opinion, Freeland may not have more than six months to live. The Oregon Death with Dignity Act defines "terminal disease" as an "incurable and irreversible disease that has been medically confirmed and will, within reasonable medical judgment, produce death *within six months*. The fact that this prognosis underestimated Michael Freeland's actual longevity by nearly two years served no protective function for this unfortunate man. He was, under the Act, technically eligible for formal medical assistance in killing himself, in lieu of, and instead of being given the protection and medical treatment he had successfully received on prior occasions.

Lethal Medication Prescribed

The physician, well known for his political activity promoting legalized assisted suicide, prescribed this distressed man a lethal overdose of federally controlled substances without so much as a cursory psychiatric examination. He did this despite the fact that the primary care doctor had diagnosed Freeland as depressed and had given him an antidepressant medication for treatment, and despite the fact that Freeland's daughter had actually asked the assisted-suicide doctor if such an examination might not be in order.

By January 23, 2002, Mr. Freeland had become so depressed and confused that a doctor hospitalized him against his will because of suicidal and possibly homicidal ideation. While efforts were made to remove his guns from his home before his discharge from the hospital, the lethal prescription was left available to him. The prescribing physician actually admitted that he had made no attempt to retrieve these lethal drugs, which were federally controlled substances, even after the Multnomah County Circuit Court determined on February 12, 2002, that Freeland was incompetent to make his own medical decisions and had appointed Freeland a temporary guardian. Under traditional notions of "legitimate medical treatment," leaving this depressed, suicidal, confused, and legally incompetent individual unsupervised, and with access to a lethal dosage of a federally controlled substance would have been considered medically negligent and unethical. Congress referred to the "[m]isuse of a drug in suicides and attempted suicides" and "injuries resulting from unsupervised use" as evidence of improper use and of drug abuse under the CSA and pointed to individuals taking controlled substances in "amounts sufficient to create a hazard to their health" as further evidence of misuse of a controlled substance and of "drug abuse." However, under the Act, Oregon does not regulate assisted suicide in the same way that it regulates medical treatments, presumably because assisted suicide cannot be, under traditional definitions, considered a medical treatment, even in Oregon.

Physicians Disagree on Appropriate Care

While pain control initially did not present a problem for Mr. Freeland, it did in the final weeks of his life. During a home visit on November 17, 2002, volunteers from Physicians for Compassionate Care Educational Foundation found that he was taking very little or no pain medication. He said that he was desperate because of the pain and was on the verge of killing himself with a prescription that had been previously provided, and disclosed that the prescribing physician had actually offered to sit with him while he took the lethal drugs. Instead, these volunteers insisted that this vulnerable and confused man be provided with the accepted standard medical care, and at the same time encouraged Mr. Freeland to take his pain medications. It was actually the volunteers who insisted that Mr. Freeland be provided with an intravenous infusion pump to administer adequate doses of opioid medications in order to control pain, and despite the fact that earlier a hospital palliative care consultant had found the need for attendant care to be a "moot point" since Mr. Freeland had available to him "life-ending medications." The consultant's comments, and the prescribing physician's deliberate failure to arrange for competent attendant care, quite clearly suggests that the availability of federally controlled substances for the purpose of facilitating Mr. Freeland's suicide actually interfered with his receiving adequate pain care, which care would otherwise have been given as consistent with the generally accepted medical standard of care and practice. Moreover, there is reason to believe that such attitudes have, in fact, contributed to the reported decrease in the adequacy of pain care among Oregon terminally ill patients since the implementation of Oregon's Death with Dignity Act. Simply stated, there was absolutely no excuse for allowing this man to suffer with untreated pain after providing him with the means of killing himself by prescribing a lethal dose of a federally controlled substance instead of pain care.

At a number of Physicians for Compassionate Care Educational Foundation palliative pain conferences, numerous experts have taught that no one needs to die in unrelieved suffering. Noted national pain care expert, Eric Chevlen, has, along with others, explained how a vast array of treatments, including long-acting opioids, everyday nonsteroidal anti-inflammatories, sophisticated spinal infusion pumps, surgical procedures, and even therapeutic radio nucleotides, along with a host of other treatments, can and will relieve the suffering of patients. . . . In every state in this country, including Oregon, and without recourse to assisted suicide, patients can receive pain care sufficient to relieve their suffering, even in the rare instance such treatment may unintentionally hasten death. In Michael Freeland's case, adequate pain care that did not hasten death was readily available, and the failure to provide that care in a timely fashion was unconscionable.

Not only was the prescription of a lethal dose of a federally controlled substance to Mr. Freeland the likely cause of his failure to receive timely and adequate pain management, the failure to treat this man's depression and suicidal despair according to locally and nationally accepted standards of medical care arose explicitly from the nature of the Oregon Death with Dignity Act and its implementing guidelines. Clearly Michael Freeland did not receive the consistent treatment of his suicidal despair that all medical standards of care require. He was not protected against access to lethal means, a crucial element in the accepted standard of practice when dealing with suicidal intentions. Instead, he was actually provided access to a lethal overdose which, outside of the Act, would have been seen as medical malpractice and unethical behavior in any state. Even in Oregon, such a practice would otherwise be considered a form of medical negligence and would have been reportable to the Board of Medical Examiners as unethical behavior, without the protections and exemptions provided for in Oregon's Death with Dignity Act. For good reason, less than 0.5% of Oregon's 10,000 doctors were found to have engaged in such behavior, which is so incompatible with the physicians role as healer.

Frightening, but not surprising, published guidelines for implementing the assisted-suicide law actually provide that, "If the mental health professional finds the patient competent, refusal of mental health treatment by the patient does not constitute a legal barrier to receiving a prescription for a lethal dose of medication" In such a case, assisted suicide is offered not as a legitimate medical and psychiatric treatment of suicidal despair as required by the rest of the country, but instead as an alternative to treatment. In every state in this country, including Oregon, the leading associations of the medical profession deem assisted suicide outside the scope of legitimate medical practice. Even the Oregon Death with Dignity Act does not define assisted suicide as a legitimate medical practice. It simply exempts that practice from the rules and regulations that otherwise define and control the practice of medicine within its boundaries.

| "Many physicians consider failure to provide assistance in dying to a patient who requests it to be abandonment of the patient."

Physician-Assisted Suicide Does Not Violate Medical Ethics

Rebecca P. Dick and Ronald A. Lindsay

In the following viewpoint Rebecca P. Dick and Ronald A. Lindsay assert that physician-assisted suicide is within the legitimate bounds of medical practice. They contend that the role of the modern physician extends beyond curing or preventing disease to relieving pain and helping patients die comfortably. Today's physicians affirm the right of a terminally ill patient to refuse life-sustaining technology and choose the manner of his or her own death. The authors argue that a physician providing controlled substances in such cases is doing so for a legitimate medical purpose. Dick and Lindsay are attorneys.

As you read, consider the following questions:

Rebecca P. Dick and Ronald A. Lindsay, *Gonzales v. Oregon*, Supreme Court of the United States, 2005.

1. According to reports filed under the Oregon Death with Dignity Act in 2004, how many patients requested lethal prescriptions?
2. Of 122 U.S. medical schools, how many administer an oath that would prohibit a physician from assisting in hastening death?
3. What terminology do the authors prefer as an alternative to physician-assisted suicide?

A physician's ongoing care for a mentally competent, terminally ill patient appropriately includes, if the patient so wishes and local law permits, assistance in enabling the patient to manage the time and manner of death. Such assistance is part of a continuum of humane medical care that begins with efforts to cure the patient and alleviate pain and suffering. If recovery becomes so unlikely that, in the patient's view, the burdens of continued attempts at a cure outweigh their benefits, then the physician redirects the course of treatment to meet the patient's wishes, while continuing to try to relieve pain and suffering. If, despite these efforts, the expected outcome is a physical or mental decline that the patient finds so repugnant, demeaning, or painful that an earlier death becomes preferable, then the physician may appropriately provide a patient who so requests with a drug to hasten death. The patient can then decide whether or not to ingest it. These forms of medical care have as their common core the physician's deep concern for the patient's well-being, informed by an understanding of the patient's convictions and most fundamental desires. In the views of many physicians practicing in the United States today and many of their patients, a physician's ability to provide assistance in hastening death is in some cases essential to effective end-of-life medical care.

Oregon's Death With Dignity Act enables patients to seek and willing physicians to provide assistance in dying after compliance with a number of procedural requirements. In providing such assistance, a physician usually prescribes a barbiturate, a Schedule II drug under the regulatory scheme established by the federal Controlled Substances Act. The Act authorizes a physician licensed under it to prescribe controlled substances listed on Schedules II–V "in the course of professional practice." Accompanying regulations permit licensed physicians to prescribe these substances for any "legitimate medical purpose." These phrases are not defined, so their meanings must be determined by reference to the context in which they are used within the overall statutory scheme. Interpreted in this manner, the terms are plainly intended to draw a distinction between drug-trafficking and patient-centered medical care. Many physicians, scholars of bioethics, and patients alike today consider physician assistance in dying for mentally competent, terminally ill patients, as permitted by Oregon's Death With Dignity Act, to be within the meaning of the statutory and regulatory language of the Controlled Substances Act. . . . Such assistance serves a legitimate medical purpose, and is a morally responsible way for the physician to respond to a competent patient's request.

Many physicians consider failure to provide assistance in dying to a patient who requests it to be abandonment of the patient just as death approaches. Continuing to aid a patient in need, indeed never abandoning a patient, is an important and long-standing principle of medical ethics. Depending on the circumstances, providing requested assistance in dying is an appropriate way for a physician to continue to address a patient's needs. . . .

The Ability to Choose Death Is Comforting

The Death With Dignity Act has proved effective, providing comfort to many while not fostering abuse. . . .

The statute, as was intended, provides invaluable hope, enhanced palliative care, and relief from anxiety for those stricken with a terminal illness. It also benefits a much larger group of Oregon residents, who are comforted by the knowledge that should their circumstances ever lead them to desire physician assistance in hastening death, they would be able to obtain it.

Speculation about possible intimidation of patients and abuse of the underprivileged has proved unfounded, according to the clear and reliable record created as a result of the statute's reporting requirements. Patients who seek prescriptions are on average better educated and more affluent than the average Oregonian. Use of hastened death has not spread in a way that might suggest lack of adequate controls; rather, the number of patients seeking prescriptions under the statute has been low—60 in 2004—and generally stable over the seven years the statute has been in effect. About one-third of the patients who obtain lethal prescriptions do not use them, confirming that the statute does not "kill" patients, but rather provides them with assistance in dying only if and when they choose it.

In addition, the statute protects against certain dangers, including underground and unregulated physician assistance in death, and painful acts of self-destruction by patients who feel trapped by their disease and compelled to kill themselves "before it is too late." In these circumstances, the statute serves to extend, not curtail, patients' lives. The Oregon statute is thus a reasonable medical and social response to the difficult end-of-life circumstances faced by some terminally ill patients. It is working as the people of Oregon intended and poses no threat to them. . . .

Medical Practice Encompasses a Range of Humane Care

The practice of medicine is a morally committed enterprise that encompasses far more than serving as a "mechanic" of bodily functions. The good physician provides the patient with comprehensive care, addressing the patient's psychological and emotional concerns as well as physical ailments. . . .

Thus, the modern physician's role is not confined exclusively to curing or preventing disease or repairing injury. Physicians assist their patients in many different ways, including genetic counseling, dietary care, assistance in reproduction, and various forms of palliative care, including hospice care. Common to all of these forms of modern care are a concern for the alleviation of pain and suffering, emotional as well as physical, and a commitment to the patient's well-being. Various forms of medical assistance aimed at such relief are now taught in medical schools throughout the United States and have gained wide acceptance in the everyday practice of medicine.

Modern views about the range of ways in which physicians should appropriately care for patients have evolved over a period of decades. Palliative and hospice care, for example, were at first controversial, because in providing such care a physician forgoes further efforts at a cure. . . . Today, however, a societal consensus has been reached and recognized in law that patients whose prospects for recovery are remote should be able to continue to obtain medical care to relieve their pain and suffering, both physical and emotional. Palliative and hospice care—although at their inception morally controversial—are now nearly universally approved. . . .

Ability to Refuse Treatment Is a Patient's Right

A patient's right to refuse use of life-sustaining technology has gained acceptance over the past thirty years. Advances in medical knowledge and technology now allow some patients to be kept alive indefinitely, even though they are in a persistent vegetative state from which there is no realistic hope of recovery. Yet many patients do not wish their lives to be prolonged in this way. The law now empowers them to make

Physicians and General Public Support Physician-Assisted Suicide

Results of a new national survey of 677 physicians and 1,057 members of the general public revealed that the majority of both groups believe that physicians should be permitted to dispense life-ending prescriptions to terminally ill patients who have made a rational decision to die due to unbearable suffering.

The national survey was conducted by HCD Research during October 6–9 [2005]. . . .

The survey indicated that nearly two-thirds of physicians (62%) and the general public (64%) believe that physicians should be permitted to dispense life-ending prescriptions.

Business Wire, *October 11, 2005.*

enforceable declarations of a desire not to be given unwanted life-sustaining care. . . .

For many terminally ill patients, palliative care and the ability to refuse treatment do not adequately address their concerns about their final days. They may face a protracted period of dying, devoid of even the simplest of pleasures, with a loss of functional capacity, possibly unremitting pain and suffering, and long hours of consciousness of the hopelessness of their condition. Many patients find this prospect unbearable. Increasingly, the medical profession and contemporary medical ethics have come to consider it appropriate to offer these patients a humane means of addressing their concerns. For some patients, this permits death with a dignity that they feel would otherwise be "denied . . . by their consciousness of dependency and helplessness as they [approach] death." . . .

In these circumstances, a physician's providing assistance in dying is not only within the legitimate bounds of medical practice, but a humane and moral response.

It would be more accurate if discussion of this medical practice were framed as "the right to die with dignity," or "hastening death," rather than as "physician-assisted suicide." When a mentally competent patient makes a choice to die during the final stages of a terminal illness there is no "suicide" in any conventional sense. The patient's act is utterly unlike the cutting short, under the influence of depression or mental confusion, of a potentially long and rewarding life. The ingestion of a controlled substance in order to accelerate death may spare the terminally ill patient much suffering, both physical pain and the anguish that, for some, accompanies helplessness and dependence. Reflecting this distinction, the Oregon statute explicitly provides that actions taken pursuant to the statute "shall not, for any purpose, constitute suicide, assisted suicide, mercy killing or homicide, under the law." . . .

Defining Legitimate Medical Practice

In arguing that assistance in hastening death is outside the scope of legitimate medical practice, some point to the Hippocratic Oath, which prohibits the giving of a "deadly drug." . . . Their views are informed more by tradition, however, than by analysis. Moreover, it is a tradition with questionable historical foundations and little viability today. This provision in the Oath, like many of its other provisions, did not reflect accepted medical practice in ancient Greek city-states, where, upon request, a physician would provide a lethal drug for a suffering patient he could not cure. More importantly, today the Hippocratic Oath is administered at only one U.S. medical school in its original form; its prohibitions on many practices integral to contemporary medicine have led to its abandonment or replacement at all other U.S. schools. Moreover, only

6 of 122 U.S. medical schools administer an oath that would prohibit physician assistance in hastening death. . . .

The Attorney General's contention that physician assistance in dying is uniformly condemned by the medical profession under all circumstances is demonstrably incorrect. And while admittedly there is some disagreement in the medical and bioethics communities about physician assistance in hastening death, this adduces nothing: many practices about which there is disagreement among professionals are clearly within "the course of professional practice." . . .

Polls, the views of physicians and others as expressed in respected medical publications, and reports of actual physician practice demonstrate that assistance in hastening death is accepted by a substantial percentage of physicians and scholars of bioethics as legitimate and humane. Thus, the practice is within "the course of professional practice," and serves a "legitimate medical purpose," as required by the Controlled Substances Act and its accompanying regulations. . . .

The Oregon Statute Offers Positive History

The Oregon statute was adopted by direct vote of the people of the state in 1994 and again in 1997. . . . It has now been in effect for more than seven years, and because of its reporting requirements, detailed information is now available about its implementation. . . . The evidence is uniformly favorable. Speculative fears about abuse have not materialized, the expected benefits have been achieved, and unanticipated advantages have been realized as well. . . .

Importantly, there is no evidence that any patient has died other than in accordance with his or her own wishes. Notably, many patients who obtain a prescription for a lethal dose of a controlled substance choose never to ingest it. In 2004 one-fifth of the 60 patients who obtained prescriptions died from natural causes, and another one-fifth were still alive at year's end. Moreover, many patients seriously consider obtaining a prescription for a lethal dose but then never choose to do so. . . . Under the statute, mentally competent, terminally ill patients remain securely in control of decision-making about their lives.

Initial concern that the statute's restrictions might be loosened in practice has not proved warranted. Use of the statute has been limited, and levels of use have remained stable. Only 208 people in the last seven years have obtained assistance in dying. The 37 deaths attributable to hastened death in 2004 amount to about one in 800 deaths among Oregonians. . . . Nor has hastened death been used primarily by individuals who might be thought vulnerable to intimidation or abuse. Those choosing assisted death had on average a higher level of education and better medical coverage than terminally ill Oregonians who did not obtain assistance in dying. The elderly, women, people with disabilities, and members of disadvantaged racial minorities have not been disproportionately affected. Only 3% of those who obtained assistance in dying were reported to have expressed concern about the financial costs of treatment. . . . There is no evidence of influence by greedy relatives, callous physicians, or profit-minded health insurers. In short, there is no evidence that the Death With Dignity Act has been a dangerous policy choice. To the contrary, it has facilitated autonomous decision-making by mentally competent, terminally ill patients at a time when they have little other control over their lives.

| "Legalization of voluntary euthanasia
cannot be regulated and that . . . leads
increasingly to involuntary euthanasia."

Physician-Assisted Suicide Leads to Abuses

Herbert Hendrin

*Herbert Hendrin is medical director of the American Foundation
for Suicide Prevention and professor of psychiatry at New York
Medical College. He is also the author of* Seduced by Death:
Doctors, Patients, and Assisted Suicide. *In the following
viewpoint Hendrin reviews the book* Euthanasia, Ethics and
Public Policy: An Argument Against Legalization, *written by
John Keown, a lecturer at Cambridge University. Hendrin praises
the book for showing how the legalization of physician-assisted
suicide in the Netherlands has led to involuntary euthanasia.
Hendrin contends that even when patients in the United States
request the removal of life support, doctors do not give them
enough time to change their minds. This shows the degree of
pressure patients will feel to end their lives should physician-
assisted suicide be legalized, he believes.*

Herbert Hendrin, "The Practice of Euthanasia," *The Hastings Center Report*, vol. 33,
July/August, 2003, pp. 44–45. Copyright © 2003 Hastings Center. Reproduced by
permission.

As you read, consider the following questions:

1. What does the court decision in *Washington v. Glucksberg* guarantee all Americans?
2. According to Hendrin, what percentage of euthanasia cases are not officially reported to the government?
3. How many involuntary deaths does the Dutch study estimate took place in 1995?

John Keown's informed and powerful argument against euthanasia features both an excellent exposition of its pitfalls and a strong confrontation with a question that remains controversial abroad: Are there circumstances in which withdrawal of treatment should be considered euthanasia? American readers of this book, who consider the question settled and are unfamiliar with cultural and legal differences in the way European countries and the United States have dealt with end-of-life issues, may be puzzled at first as to why this University of Cambridge lecturer in the law and ethics of medicine wants to address this question. But Keown's exposition will make even such readers, who believe we have wisely avoided many of the dilemmas Great Britain and other European countries are forced to face, realize that there are some dilemmas we have not escaped.

To evaluate euthanasia, Keown examines its actual practice. He carefully provides evidence to show that legalization of voluntary euthanasia cannot be regulated and that it leads increasingly to involuntary euthanasia and to patients who are not ready to die or whose suffering could be alleviated by palliative medicine. Such a study relies heavily on the Dutch experience, since not only has the practice been legal in the Netherlands for some time, but two Dutch government-sanctioned studies (in 1990 and 1995), in which physicians participated anonymously and with impunity, have shown us what the actual practice entails.

No Informed Consent

The Dutch studies play down a fact they cannot help but reveal, namely, that thousands of patients have their lives ended without their consent. The studies report 3,600 deaths in 1995 from assisted suicide and euthanasia and officially acknowledge between 900 and 1,000 involuntary deaths. But they refuse to describe as euthanasia, or involuntary (when a competent patient does not give consent) or nonvoluntary (when the patient is deemed unable to give consent) euthanasia, the 1,350 patients in 1990 or the close to 2,000 patients in 1995 whose physicians gave them large doses of pain-killing medication with the primary aim of ending their lives. In the course of my own studies of euthanasia in the Netherlands, I asked Paul Van Der Maas, the principal investigator of the Dutch government-sanctioned studies, why, if patients had consented to the drug overdose, these should not be considered euthanasia cases. He conceded they could be—the only difference was that the patients took longer to die. When asked why, if patients were put to death who had not consented (about a third of the patients), these cases were not considered nonvoluntary or involuntary euthanasia, Van der Maas could not give a reason, but he was not willing to consider recategorizing them.

When one realizes that in one-quarter of the cases in which Dutch physicians give medications intending to end patients' lives, they do so without the patient's consent, that a third of Dutch doctors admit to having done so, that half of Dutch doctors feel free to suggest euthanasia to their patients, and that 60 percent of Dutch euthanasia cases are not reported to the authorities, one is inclined to agree with Keown that this is a system out of control.

Feeding Tube Withdrawals

Keown is also concerned, however, that the data on the many thousands of Dutch cases where treatment (including tube

Eliminating the Sufferer

When suffering can be eliminated by eliminating the sufferer, the Dutch are likely to question why they should expend precious health care funds, and limited tax monies, to care for those who are chronically or terminally ill.

The Christian Century, *May 2, 2001.*

feeding) was withdrawn without patient consent do not permit us to know whether the doctor was merely stopping a futile or burdensome treatment or intended instead to end the patient's life—referred to as "passive euthanasia." This is an issue that has also troubled Keown in his own country because British law since the landmark *Bland* case has condoned passive euthanasia. Most of the concluding chapters of Keown's book deal with his concern with passive euthanasia and reflect some of the differences in approach to end of life care between Europe and the United States.

In 1989, Tony Bland was left in a persistent vegetative state after being crushed by a crowd at a soccer game. His parents and his doctor wished to stop his tube feeding and antibiotics. The hospital where Bland was receiving treatment applied for and received permission from the High Court to do so. The Official Solicitor—whom the court designates in such cases to represent the patient—appealed to a committee of the House of Lords, claiming that discontinuation should be considered murder, or at least manslaughter. The Law Lords rejected an appeal by the solicitor, distinguishing the case from homicide since what was involved was an act of omission, not commission. Since the doctors' intent was admittedly to end the patient's life, Keown asks why that should not be considered euthanasia. The decision in this and other withdrawal of treatment cases Keown describes are often essentially quality of life decisions with the courts accepting "responsible" medical opinion as to what was in the patient's best interests or when a life was not worth preserving.

In this country, the Supreme Court recognized in *Washington v. Glucksberg* that patients have a "constitutionally protected right to refuse lifesaving hydration and nutrition." The right to withdraw from treatment is considered no different from the right to forgo treatment in the first place. The Court cited the common law rule that forced treatment is "battery"—an invasion of a patient's bodily integrity. In most states a living will or a family member or guardian can exercise these protections for incompetent patients. This approach has enabled patients to live as they wish at the end of their lives without regard to a physician's intentions. Not making the decision rest on the distinction between commissions or omission has served us well.

All Rights Are Conditional

Nevertheless, some of the questions Keown raises are also unresolved in the United States. He does not believe, for example, that the patients' wishes should categorically determine withdrawal of treatment. What if a disabled person dependent on a ventilator becomes depressed and suicidal and wants it disconnected? Do we not at least first treat the depression? Or what of individuals who become quadriplegic and, at least initially, are totally dependent on ventilators and want them disconnected? Some hospitals simply follow the law literally and disconnect them. Others, recognizing that such patients usually, as they are partially weaned from the respirator, change their minds, give them time to do so. Disability rights advocates in this country are outraged over our tendency to assume that it is "natural" for the severely disabled to want to end their lives.

In 1999, the British Medical Association published a guide for physicians about withholding and withdrawing medical treatment, including tubal nutrition. The guide endorsed withholding tube-delivered food and water from non-terminally ill patients with severe dementia. Since such treatment accomplishes its purpose, Keown points out that, as in the *Bland* case, the decision reflects the notion that the patient, not the treatment, is considered not worthwhile. This is a principle contradictory to traditional medical ethics. No medical or social consensus had been reached in the United States regarding treatment in such cases, particularly when families and physicians are not in agreement.

The power of Keown's argument holds your interest while making you think. His analysis of euthanasia in the Netherlands, of its brief legalization in Australia, and of assisted suicide in Oregon is a strikingly perceptive treatment of the subject from a European perspective. The lucidity of Keown's logic make this book a provocative and important contribution to the ethical and public policy issues involved in end-of-life care.

> *"It is premature to judge that
> . . . regulations cannot effectively
> protect patients from serious abuses of
> the legal right to physician-assisted
> suicide."*

Abuse of Physician-Assisted Suicide Can Be Prevented

Carl Wellman

Well-crafted state statutes can prevent any abuse of physician-assisted suicide, argues Carl Wellman in the following viewpoint. For example, statutes could require that suicide requests be made on separate occasions over a period of time, that they be given freely without undue influence, and that they not be the result of depression or mental illness, he claims. In addition, Wellman asserts, physicians must be required to first provide pain-relief alternatives, and state authorities must oversee and enforce all regulations. Wellman is professor of philosophy and the humanities at Washington University in St. Louis.

As you read, consider the following questions:

    1. Under what conditions do patients have no moral duty

Carl Wellman, "A Legal Right to Physician-Assisted Suicide Defended," *Social Theory and Practice*, vol. 29, no. 1, January 2003, pp. 19–38. Copyright © 2003 by Florida State University. Reproduced by permission of the publisher and the author.

to refrain from suicide, in Wellman's view?

2. According to the author, what are some of the ways in which physician-assisted suicide might be abused?

3. In the author's opinion, what reassuring evidence has emerged since the enactment of Oregon's Death with Dignity Act?

There ought to be a right to physician-assisted suicide [PAS] under United States law unless it is necessary to deny this right to patients who are terminally ill or enduring intolerable unrelievable suffering in order to prevent some great social harm or to promote an important state interest. Let us examine the most plausible arguments of those who believe that this is so.

A Right to Life

It is necessary to prohibit physician-assisted suicide in order to promote the important state interest in the preservation of human life. Although I readily grant that every state does have an important interest in the preservation of human life, I doubt that this rules out the right to physician-assisted suicide. Why do states have an interest in preserving human lives? One reason is that there is a human right to life and the state ought to protect the human rights of its subjects. So far, so good, but how does this apply to physician-assisted suicide? Many argue that suicide is self-murder and thus any patient who exercised her right to physician-assisted suicide would violate her own right to life. It is hard to know how to assess this reasoning because the human right to life is often asserted but seldom defined. I believe that the human right to life is a rights-package including at least the individual's claim-right not to be killed by others. Correlative to this claim is the duty of others not to kill one. But because the notion of a moral claim against oneself makes no sense, killing oneself is not an analogous violation of one's own human right to life. However,

I also believe that moral agents have a general duty, a duty under normal circumstances, not to commit suicide. But at least in the case of patients suffering intolerable unrelievable suffering, this duty is undermined by excessive sacrifice. There are limits to moral obligation. Although a firefighter has a duty to enter a burning building to rescue a resident, she does not have any duty to do so when the building is about to collapse and any attempt to rescue would mean certain death. Similarly, patients have no moral duty to refrain from suicide when this would mean intolerable suffering.

Still, one's physician could easily refrain from assisting a patient to commit suicide and arguably ought to do so because assisting a patient to commit suicide is killing that patient, thus violating her claim-right not to be killed by another. But the physician does not kill the patient by providing her with the means to kill herself. If the patient chooses to use these means to commit suicide, it is the patient who does the killing. Nor is the physician an accomplice in an immoral killing, because the qualified patient has no moral duty not to commit suicide. In any event, the patient will have waived any moral rights holding against the physician by requesting her assistance. Granted that the human right to life is inalienable, waiving a right is not alienating it. The patient retains her right to life, as evidenced by the fact that if some misguided stranger were to kill the patient, he would be violating her right to life. . . .

The Argument that PAS Causes Abuses

[Many opponents argue that] there ought not to be any legal right to physician-assisted suicide because any such right would be seriously abused. For one thing, it would cause right-holders who would prefer to live to be pressured, even coerced, into committing physician-assisted suicide against their wills. Family members under emotional and financial

Public Laws Will Protect Against the "Slippery Slope"

Life itself is precariously poised on a "slippery slope." We cannot avoid life's "slippery slopes." . . . So we provide laws as guidelines and safeguards to draw lines and to anchor us. Hikers and climbers sometimes cross steep, icy and snowy, slippery slopes. They rope together and draw a line of travel along the best but least risky route. They set anchors into the snow and ice to insure safety. When aid-in-dying is legalized, lines will be drawn between individual rights and public safety. Public laws will set legal anchors to insure against slides down the "slippery slope."

Rob Neils, "Death With Dignity FAQs."
www.togopeacefully.com.

strain would be sorely tempted to talk a patient into exercising his right to commit physician-assisted suicide. Even the most loving and conscientious family members might well rationalize that death would be best for the patient. Health care institutions vigorously pursuing cost containment and mindful of the disproportionate amount of medical resources allocated to patients during the last year of their lives might refuse to finance medical care desired by those qualified to exercise the right to physician-assisted suicide. Even physicians, many of whom are dedicated to curing illness and overcoming disability and are reluctant to care for patients they think of as hopeless, might unintentionally exert undue influence by the way they present their diagnoses and explain the prognosis to patients qualified to commit physician-assisted suicide.

Also [critics allege] any legal right to physician-assisted suicide would result in discrimination against the vulnerable.

Our stereotypes condition us to undervalue the lives of several categories of persons, especially the poor, the elderly, the mentally ill, and the disabled or handicapped. We imagine that, unfortunately, none of them can live as productive, rewarding, and enjoyable lives as normal persons. It might seem merciful to inform them of their right to commit physician-assisted suicide and encourage them to exercise this right. Members of these groups are less able than others to resist such pressures and would in practice end their lives prematurely in disproportionate numbers.

Finally, [the anti-PAS argument goes] the existence of a legal right to physician-assisted suicide would lead physicians to provide lethal medication to unqualified patients. It would in practice be impossible to confine physician-assisted suicide to patients who are terminally ill or enduring intolerable un-relievable suffering. The concept of terminal illness involves a prediction that, given the variability of individual cases, can never be certain, and the concept of suffering is so subjective that there are no objective measures of the degree of suffering. Hence, attending physicians would often provide lethal medication to patients whose illness could be at least partially reversed and to demanding patients whose suffering is not intolerable, perhaps not even especially severe. Presumably, only a patient who is competent to make a rational decision would possess any right to physician-assisted suicide. But patients who are seriously ill or enduring suffering tend to become depressed, and the major cause of premature suicide is depression. Physicians are not professionally qualified to distinguish between mild depression that leaves a patient capable of making a rational decision and a deeper depression that renders a patient legally incompetent. Hence, once again physicians would often provide assistance to suicidal patients who do not possess any legal right to physician-assisted suicide.

Insufficient Evidence of Abuses

To my mind, and that of many others, the danger of abuse is the strongest argument against having any legal right to physician-assisted suicide under United States law. Each of these abuses is possible and highly undesirable. The question, and it is an empirical question, is how often they would in fact occur. To date there is insufficient empirical evidence to answer this question with any confidence. Interpretations of the studies of physician-assisted suicide in the Netherlands, where it has been practiced for several years, reach conflicting conclusions. Moreover, the relevance of these studies of medical practices in a jurisdiction that permits euthanasia as well as physician-assisted suicide to the proposal to introduce only physician-assisted suicide remains in doubt. Here in our country, it is too early to draw any reliable conclusions about the dangers of the Oregon Death With Dignity Act. However, some of the evidence is reassuring. Fewer patients have requested lethal medication from their physicians than was anticipated, and a considerable number of patients who have obtained such medication have chosen not to use it to commit suicide but have died of natural causes. One advantage of introducing this right by legislation in the several states, rather than by a decision of the United States Supreme Court, is that the states would enact somewhat different protective regulations. This would over time provide empirical evidence of whether most serious abuses of the legal right to physician-assisted suicide can be prevented and, if so, how to do so most effectively.

My semi-educated guess is that the kinds of abuses mentioned above can be held to an acceptable minimum. Some guidance on how this might be accomplished can be found in "A Model State Act to Authorize and Regulate Physician-Assisted Suicide" proposed by Charles H. Baron and others. In addition to specifying the conditions necessary for a patient to possess the right to physician-assisted suicide, this model statute specifies that a physician is permitted to provide lethal medication only if the patient has made a request that is not the result of clinical depression or any other mental illness, represents the patient's reasoned choice, has been made free of undue influence, and has been repeated without self-contradiction on two separate occasions at least fourteen days apart. Moreover, before providing medical means of suicide, the physician must offer to the patient all available medical care, including hospice care, secure a written opinion from a consulting physician that the patient is suffering from a terminal illness or an intractable and unbearable illness, and secure a written opinion from a psychiatrist, clinical psychologist, or psychiatric social worker that the patient's request is not the result of any distortion of the patient's judgment due to clinical depression or any other mental illness. There are also requirements concerning documentation and reporting to enable medical institutions and state authorities to oversee and enforce these and other regulations. It is premature to judge that some such set of regulations cannot effectively protect patients from serious abuses of the legal right to physician-assisted suicide. . . .

A Cry for Reform

I conclude that each of the several states ought to enact a right to physician-assisted suicide. It would be useful for the various state statutes to differ in details, especially regarding protective regulations, in order to obtain empirical evidence concerning the least dangerous and most beneficial formulation. Still, all of the rights conferred should have the same basic structure. They should be possessed by all and only those patients who are either enduring intolerable unrelievable suffering or terminally ill. They should be rights-packages consisting of three liberty-rights—the rights to request or not request, to obtain or not obtain, and to use or not use assistance provided by one's physician to commit suicide. In addition to its defining core bilateral liberty, each of these rights must include associated elements that confer dominion, freedom, and control over this liberty upon the right-holder. Among these will be the legal liberty of the attending physician to provide, subject to protective regulations, requested medical assistance to her patient.

I do not take the arguments against enacting a legal right to physician-assisted suicide lightly. They are serious arguments, both because they concern important public interests and because there is not yet sufficient empirical evidence to predict reliably how much, if at all, any such right would damage those interests. Nevertheless, I have explained why I do not believe that they outweigh the reasons in favor of enacting a legal right to physician-assisted suicide. These are to enable qualified patients to avoid unnecessary suffering, to enable them to die with dignity, to avoid intruding into their lives, and to respect their rational agency. These compelling moral considerations cry out for the reform of United States law to make it less inhumane and more just.

"Each individual has the right to decide the hour of his death and to implement that solemn decision as best he can."

Physician-Assisted Suicide Is a Moral Right

Thomas A. Bowden

According to Thomas A. Bowden in the following viewpoint, the U.S. Constitution grants Americans the right to life, liberty, and the pursuit of happiness. Inherent in these rights is the right to decide when one's life should end, he maintains. The law should not stand in the way of physicians who, based on their sound judgment, choose to help suffering individuals exercise their right to suicide, Bowden argues. Thomas A. Bowden is an attorney and writer for the Ayn Rand Institute.

As you read, consider the following questions:

1. What does Bowden think the Supreme Court should do in its review of the Oregon physician-assisted suicide law?

2. In the author's view, how does declaring that society

must give you permission to kill yourself contradict the right to life?

3. Why is suicide anathema to religious conservatives, in the author's opinion?

In upholding Oregon's physician-assisted suicide law, the Supreme Court reached the right result for the wrong reasons.

Since 1997 Oregon physicians have been permitted by statute to help their patients commit suicide. On Tuesday the Supreme Court upheld this controversial law, reaching the right result for the wrong reasons. By basing its decision on legal technicalities, the Court managed to avoid addressing the real issue: an individual's unconditional right to commit suicide.

The Oregon law permits a doctor to prescribe a lethal dose of drugs to a mentally competent, terminally ill patient who makes written and oral requests, consults two physicians, and endures a mandatory waiting period. The patient's relatives and doctors are powerless to engage in legalized "mercy killing," as they cannot apply on the patient's behalf, and the patient himself administers the lethal dose.

Why the Case Reached the Supreme Court

In 2001 Attorney General John Ashcroft decreed that any doctor prescribing such a dose would violate federal law against dispensing controlled dangerous substances without a "legitimate medical purpose." Consequently, the case reached the Supreme Court as a technical debate between federal and state governments over which one should regulate the practice of medicine. On Tuesday the Court ruled that the state of Oregon could permit assisted suicide, despite the federal law.

But who was missing from that debate? The individual patients whose lives were at stake.

What the Supreme Court should have done was bypass legal technicalities and revisit its 1997 decision in *Washington*

The Role of the State

[Philosopher] John Stuart Mill argued in *On Liberty* that the sole purpose for which the state can rightly exercise power over an individual is to prevent harm to others. "His own good, either physical or moral," Mill wrote, "is not a sufficient warrant." A century and a half later, . . . we tend to agree that the state should not seek to impose its own conception of what is morally right on individuals who are not harming others. One of the implications of this principle is that the state should not prevent people who are terminally or incurably ill from ending their lives when they see fit.

Peter Singer, Free Inquiry, *February/March 2005.*

v. Glucksberg, which held that individuals have no constitutionally protected right of suicide, and hence no right to obtain assistance in that act.

The Government Has No Right to Prevent Suicide

What the courts must grasp, if they are ever to resolve the battle over assisted suicide once and for all, is that there is no rational, secular basis upon which the government can properly prevent any individual from choosing to end his own life. When religious conservatives use secular laws to enforce their idea of God's will, they threaten the central principle on which America was founded.

The Declaration of Independence proclaimed, for the first time in the history of nations, that each person exists as an end in himself. This basic truth—which finds political expression in the right to life, liberty, and the pursuit of happiness—means, in practical terms, that you need no one's permission to live, and that no one may forcibly obstruct your efforts to achieve your own personal happiness.

But what if happiness becomes impossible to attain? What if a dread disease, or some other calamity, drains all joy from life, leaving only misery and suffering? The right to life includes and implies the right to commit suicide. To hold otherwise—to declare that society must give you permission to kill yourself—is to contradict the right to life at its root. If you have a duty to go on living, despite your better judgment, then your life does not belong to you, and you exist by permission, not by right.

An Individual's Right to Decide

For these reasons, each individual has the right to decide the hour of his death and to implement that solemn decision as best he can. The choice is his because the life is his. And if a doctor is willing to assist in the suicide, based on an objective assessment of his patient's mental and physical state, the law should not stand in his way.

Religious conservatives' outrage at the Oregon law stems from the belief that human life is a gift from the Lord, who puts us here on earth to carry out His will. Thus, the very idea of suicide is anathema, because one who "plays God" by causing his own death, or assisting in the death of another, insults his Maker and invites eternal damnation, not to mention divine retribution against the decadent society that permits such sinful behavior.

If George W. Bush were to contract a terminal disease, he would have a legal right to regard his own God's will as paramount, and to instruct his doctor to stand by and let him suffer, just as long as his body and mind could endure the agony, until the last bitter paroxysm carried him to the grave. But the Bush administration has no right to force such mindless, medieval misery upon doctors and patients who refuse to regard their precious lives as playthings of a cruel God.

Conservatives crave to inject religion into the bloodstream of American law, thereby assisting in our own national suicide. However, they cannot succeed without the Supreme Court's consent. Sooner or later, the Court must confront the main issue, and decide whether an individual's right to life includes the right to commit suicide.

| "What advocates of 'death with dignity' want is to overcome our cultivated horror . . . of suicide by giving the decision to self-destruct a quasi-medical veneer."

Physician-Assisted Suicide Legitimizes Self-Destruction

Maggie Gallagher

In the following viewpoint Maggie Gallagher maintains that laws condoning physician-assisted suicide give social approval to suicide. Those who support such laws hope to overcome Americans' aversion to suicide by making it appear to be a medical decision, she asserts. Making suicide a legal choice, Gallagher argues, makes it a moral option and tells the sick, the elderly, and other vulnerable people that their lives have no value. Gallagher is a syndicated columnist and affiliate scholar at the Institute for American Values.

As you read, consider the following questions:

1. According to Gallagher, why is the number of people affected by Oregon's physician-assisted suicide law

Maggie Gallagher, "Assisted Suicide Gives Medical Credence to Self-Destruction," Townhall.com, June 2, 2004. Copyright © 2004 Universal Press Syndicate. Reproduced with permission of Universal Press Syndicate.

greater than the number of facilitated suicides?

2. In the author's opinion, why are the official death certificates lies?

3. Why does the author believe that no law can give or take away the choice to commit suicide?

Oregon is the only state in the union that facilitates suicide. *The New York Times'* Science section touts the virtues of the assisted suicide law, which since 1997 has facilitated at least 171 suicides.

The number of people affected by the law is, of course, much larger, whether it is old people comforted by the idea that they can kill themselves, or families forced into intimate discussions of when might be a good time for Grandma to kill herself.

If your father is old and sick in Oregon, the subject of suicide becomes part of the family discussion. Your cousin will raise it as you try together to glimpse the future. Your mom may share her feelings about it with you as she works through the implications of her newfound legal right. If you refuse to treat suicide as a normal possibility, you may be stigmatized as lacking in compassion or respect for her rights. If suicide is a legal choice, then it is a moral option. Thinking through moral options together, that's what families do, right?

Declaring Lives Worthless

Worse, legal approval of suicide amounts to a declaration to the old, sick and vulnerable that others consider their lives worthless. Dr. Kenneth Stephens, chairman of the department of radiation oncology at the Oregon Health and Science University in Portland (who heads Physicians for Compassionate Care), related how his own wife reacted when, as she struggled with cancer, her doctor offered her an overdose of drugs: "He wants me to kill myself," she told her husband. "It just devastated her that her doctor, her trusted doctor, subtly suggested that," Stephens told *The New York Times.*

Society Condemns Assisted Suicide

The judgment that there is no form of criminal punishment acceptable for a completed suicide and that the threat of criminal punishment is singularly inefficacious in deterring attempts to commit suicide does not mean that there is a "right" to commit the act. Nor does it mean that one has a justified claim that others must or should provide assistance in committing the act. Indeed, society can do something about those who aid someone else to commit suicide—and it has. Throughout our history we have directed the force of the criminal law against aiding or assisting suicide or soliciting another to do so.

Yale Kamisar, First Things,
December 1993.

In one case on record, an HMO prescribed an elderly woman lethal drugs in spite of one psychiatrist's observation that it was her daughter, more than the mother, who wanted it. More than a third of patients, according to the *Times,* cite fear of burdening their families as a reason for their request.

How common are cases like this? To keep horror out of the headlines, information about assisted suicide in Oregon is tightly controlled, as Wesley Smith pointed out in *The Weekly Standard.*

The official death certificates are lies, required by law to list the underlying illness as the cause of death, not the actual suicide. Patients are supposed to be mentally competent and within six months of death, but at a recent meeting of the American Psychiatric Association, a psychiatrist disclosed that a patient was prescribed the poison pill despite being diagnosed as having "depressive disorder," "intermittent delirium" and even after "being declared mentally incompetent by a court," according to Smith.

This patient fortunately called Physicians for Compassionate Care instead of swallowing the poison. He died more than a year later, properly treated for depression, with good pain control, surrounded by people who reassured him his life was valuable. With the time he had left, he reconciled with his estranged daughter.

Which is the better, freer, more compassionate society? No law can give or take away the choice to commit suicide. Guns, poisons, noxious fumes, trains—there is simply no way to stop suicide in people healthy enough to swallow. (Oregon's law requires the patient to self-administer his own poison.)

What Oregon's suicide laws actually do is convey social approval to individuals contemplating self-destruction, and to their friends and relatives. What advocates of "death with dignity" want is to overcome our cultivated horror at the idea of suicide by giving the decision to self-destruct a quasi-medical veneer.

Periodical Bibliography

Peter D. Browning — "Community Care of the Dying: Beyond the Euthanasia Debate," *Encounter*, Winter 2005.

David B. Fletcher — "Holy Dying, Assisted Dying? An Anglican Perspective on Physician-Assisted Suicide," *Ethics and Medicine*, Spring 2004.

Faye Girsh — "Ashcroft, Eastwood, and Assisted Dying," *Humanist*, May/June 2005.

Jonathan Jones — "Religious Scholars Weigh in on Assisted Suicide," *Oakland Tribune*, October 9, 2005.

Patricia Lefevere and Robert McClory — "Schiavo Autopsy Points Up Need for End-of-Life Discussions," *National Catholic Reporter*, July 1, 2005.

Rita L. Marker — "Assisted-Suicide Activism: Patience and Plastic Bags," *Human Life Review*, Spring 2003.

Oregon Department of Human Services — "Seventh Annual Report on Oregon's Death with Dignity Act," March 10, 2005. http://egov.oregon.gov.

Pew Research Center for the People and the Press — "Strong Support for Right to Die," January 5, 2006. http://people-press.org.

Dennis Sullivan — "Euthanasia Versus Letting Die: Christian Decision-Making in Terminal Patients," *Ethics and Medicine*, Summer 2005.

For Further Discussion

Chapter 1

1. Caitlin Borgmann argues that the right to abortion is necessary in order for women to have equal protection under the law. Do you agree or disagree? Cite specific examples from Borgmann's arguments and your reason for agreement or disagreement.

2. Frances Kissling supports a woman's right to decide whether or not to continue a pregnancy. Charles I. Lugosi argues that the fetus has civil rights separate from those of the mother. What might be some long-range implications if judicial precedence were to establish that a fetus has constitutional rights independent from those of the mother?

3. Antony Barone Kolenc considers the partial-birth abortion procedure infanticide rather than abortion. What is the difference between these two terms? Which term do you believe applies most accurately to partial-birth abortion, and why?

Chapter 2

1. Robert Grant views the death penalty as a violent act that breeds further violence. Iain Murray sees the death penalty as a deterrent to violent crime. What types of information or statistics are needed to truly assess the impact of the death penalty on crime? Cite examples from the viewpoints where appropriate.

2. After reading the viewpoints by Jeffrey M. Jones and Anna Badkhen, what factor do you think most influences public opinion about the death penalty? Cite information from the viewpoints to support your answer.

3. The Supreme Court decided in *Roper v. Simmons* that the death penalty should not be applied to juveniles under age eighteen. Sasha Abramsky supports this decision while Sandra Day O'Connor opposes it. Do you think the Court's decision was right or wrong? Cite the facts from these two viewpoints that were most convincing to you.

Chapter 3

1. David C. Grossman et al. argues that safe gun storage practices can reduce teen suicide rates. In contrast, Joseph P. Tartaro claims that teen suicide rates are exaggerated, making such practices unnecessary. Which author do you find most persuasive, and why?

2. Robert Li Kitts asserts that homosexuality increases the risk of teen suicide, but Ritch C. Savin-Williams and Geoffrey L. Ream disagree with this claim. Kitts examines multiple studies conducted over many years to back up his argument, while Savin-Williams and Ream describe the results of their own study to support their contentions. Which do you think uses research studies to the best effect, Kitts or Savin-Williams and Ream?

Chapter 4

1. Physicians for Compassionate Care Educational Foundation (PCCEF) argues that it would be a violation of medical ethics for physicians to aid terminally ill patients in dying. On the other hand, Rebecca P. Dick and Ronald A. Lindsay contend that physician-assisted suicide does not violate medical ethics. Which do you think makes the best argument, PCCEF or Dick and Lindsay?

2. Herbert Hendrin claims that physician-assisted suicide would naturally lead to abuses, but Carl Wellman argues that regulations on the practice can prevent them. Hendrin is the medical director of the American Foundation for Suicide Prevention and a professor of psychiatry. Wellman

is a philosophy and humanities professor. How does knowing their credentials help in evaluating their arguments?

Organizations to Contact

American Association of Suicidology (AAS)

5221 Wisconsin Ave. NW, Washington, DC 20015

(202) 237-2280 • fax: (202) 237-2282

e-mail: info@suicidology.org

Web site: www.suicidology.org

The goal of the AAS is to understand and prevent suicide through promotion of research, public awareness programs, public education, and training for professionals and volunteers. In addition, AAS serves as a national clearinghouse for information on suicide. The association publishes *Suicide and Life-Threatening Behavior*, AAS's bimonthly journal *Newslink*, a quarterly newsletter for members called *Surviving Suicide*, a quarterly newsletter for survivors entitled *Annual Conference Proceedings*, and the *Directory of Suicide Prevention and Crisis Intervention Agencies in the U.S.* The National Suicide Prevention Lifeline, 1-800-273-TALK, provides access to trained telephone counselors, twenty-four hours a day, seven days a week.

American Foundation for Suicide Prevention (AFSP)

120 Wall St., 22nd Floor, New York, NY 10005

(212) 363-3500 • fax: (212) 363-6237

e-mail: inquiry@afsp.org

Web site: www.afsp.org

The American Foundation for Suicide Prevention funds research, develops prevention initiatives, and offers educational programs and conferences for suicide survivors, mental health professionals, physicians, and the public. AFSP opposes the legalization of physician-assisted suicide. The organization's Web site provides information on current suicide research, suicide prevention awareness events, and links to local AFSP chapters and other related organizations.

The American Geriatrics Society/Association of Directors of Geriatric Academic Programs (AGS)
Empire State Building, 350 Fifth Ave., Suite 801, New York, NY 10118
(212) 308-1414, ext. 303 • fax: (212) 832-8646
e-mail: lkahn@americangeriatrics.org
Web site: www.americangeriatrics.org

The American Geriatrics Society is the professional organization of health care providers dedicated to improving the health and well-being of all older adults. With an active membership of over sixty-eight hundred health care professionals, the AGS has a long history of effecting change in the provision of health care for older adults. In the last decade the society has worked at shaping attitudes, policies, and practices regarding health care for older people. The American Geriatrics Society has issued a statement on physician-assisted suicide and voluntary active euthanasia on its Web site.

American Life League (ALL)
PO Box 1350, Stafford, VA 22555
(540) 659-4171 • fax: (540) 659-2586
e-mail: jbrown@all.org
Web site: www.all.org

The American Life League opposes all forms of artificial birth control and supports sex education only when based on absolute standards of right and wrong. ALL opposes abortion and embraces the opinion that abortion can never be necessary to save the life of the mother. ALL opposes mercy killing, euthanasia, and physician-assisted suicide, and rejects the argument that there is a constitutional "right to die." The organization publishes the bimonthly pro-life magazine *Celebrate Life*, a monthly current events newsletter the *Ryan Report*, and a weekly online news update *Communiqué*.

Amnesty International USA
5 Penn Plaza, New York, NY 10001
(212) 807-8400 • fax: (212) 627-1451
e-mail: aimember@aiusa.org

Web site: www.amnestyusa.org

Amnesty International seeks to free all prisoners of conscience, to ensure a prompt and fair trial for all political prisoners, to abolish the death penalty and torture, to end extrajudicial executions and "disappearances," and to ensure that perpetrators of such abuses are brought to justice in accordance with international standards. The orgnization's Web site offers a variety of information on the use of the death penalty worldwide.

Catholics for a Free Choice
1436 U St. NW, Suite 301, Washington, DC   20009-3997
(202) 986-6093 • fax: (202) 332-7995
e-mail: cffc@catholicsforchoice.org
Web site: www.catholicsforchoice.org

CFFC supports the right to legal abortion. The organization promotes family planning to reduce the incidence of abortion and increase women's choices in childbearing and child rearing. The organization's Web site offers a number of articles and publications, including *Catholics and Abortion: Notes on Canon Law No. 1.*

Compassion and Choices
PO Box 101810, Denver, CO   80250-1810
(800) 247-7421 • fax: (303) 639-1224
e-mail: info@compassionandchoices.org
Web site: www.compassionandchoices.org

Formerly known as the Hemlock Society, the organization changed its name in 2003 to End-of-Life Choices and in 2004 merged with Compassion in Dying to become Compassion and Choices. The organization is dedicated to providing access to privacy, choice, dignity, and autonomy in end-of-life care decisions. It supports comprehensive palliative care, with legal assisted death as an alternative if suffering is unbearable. Its *Compassion and Choices Magazine* is available quarterly to members, and the current issue is available on the organization's Web site.

The Compassionate Friends

PO Box 3696, Oak Brook, IL   60522-3696
(877) 969-0010 • fax: (630) 990-0246
Web site: www.compassionatefriends.org

The Compassionate Friends is a national nonprofit, self-help support organization that offers friendship, understanding, and hope to bereaved parents, grandparents, and siblings. The organization is not affiliated with any religion and charges no membership dues or fees. The mission of The Compassionate Friends is to assist families toward the positive resolution of grief following the death of a child of any age and to provide information to help others be supportive.

Death with Dignity National Center (DDNC)

520 SW Sixth Ave., Suite 1030, Portland, OR   97204
(503) 228-4415 • fax: (503) 228-7454
e-mail: info@deathwithdignity.org
Web site: www.deathwithdignity.org

DDNC provides information, education, research, and support for the preservation, implementation, and promotion of the Oregon Death with Dignity law to stimulate nationwide improvements in end-of-life care. The center works for the rights of all Americans to make well-informed decisions with their physicians and loved ones about their end-of-life care. DDNC advocates improved end-of-life pain management and palliative care. Publications available on the organization's Web site include the *Dignity Report* newsletter and the *Improvements in End-of-Life Care* report.

Depression and Bipolar Support Alliance (DBSA)

730 N. Franklin St., Suite 501, Chicago, IL   60610-7224
(800) 826-3632 • fax: (312) 642-7243
Web site: www.dbsalliance.org

The Depression and Bipolar Support Alliance is the nation's leading patient-directed organization focusing on the most prevalent mental illnesses—depression and bipolar disorder.

The organization fosters understanding of the impact and management of these life-threatening illnesses by providing up-to-date, scientifically based tools and information written in language the general public can understand. DBSA supports research to promote more timely diagnosis, develop more effective and tolerable treatments, and discover a cure. The organization works to ensure that people living with mood disorders are treated equitably.

Euthanasia Research and Guidance Organization
24829 Norris Ln., Junction City, OR   97448-9559
e-mail: ergo@efn.org
Web site: www.finalexit.org

The Euthanasia Research and Guidance Organization, a nonprofit educational corporation based in Oregon, was founded in 1993 to improve the quality of background research concerning assisted dying for persons who are terminally or hopelessly ill and wish to end their suffering. ERGO holds that voluntary euthanasia, physician-assisted suicide, and self-deliverance are all appropriate life endings depending on the individual and medical and ethical circumstances. As well as conducting opinion polls, ERGO develops and publishes guidelines—ethical, psychological, and legal—for patients and physicians to better prepare them to make life-ending decisions. The organization supplies literature to, and does research for, other right-to-die groups worldwide, and it briefs journalists, authors, and graduate students who are coming fresh to the issue.

Feminists for Life of America (FFL)
733 Fifteenth St. NW, Suite 1100, Washington, DC   20005
(202) 737-3352
e-mail: info@feministsforlife.org
Web site: www.feministsforlife.org

FFL is a pro-life organization that supports education, life planning, and mentoring programs for girls and women of all ages. FFL is dedicated to eliminating the root causes that drive women to abortion—primarily lack of practical resources and support. FFL opposes euthanasia as devaluing the lives of disabled persons. A variety of publications are available on the organization's Web site. Materials on the site are generally geared to a college-age audience.

Friends for Survival
PO Box 214463, Sacramento, CA   95821
(916) 392-0664
Web site: www.friendsforsurvival.org

Friends for Survival is an organization of people who have been affected by a death caused by suicide. It is dedicated to providing a variety of peer support services that comfort those in grief, encourage healing and growth, foster the development of skills to cope with a loss, and educate the entire community regarding the impact of suicide. The outreach of Friends for Survival volunteers can bridge the gap between despair and renewed hope. Those whose loss is recent can lean upon the shoulders of those who have made progress in the difficult task of working through grief.

Human Life International (HLI)
4 Family Life Ln., Front Royal, VA   22630
(800) 549-5433 • fax: (540) 622-6247
e-mail: hli@hli.org
Web site: www.hli.org

HLI is a pro-life organization that rejects abortion, contraception, and euthanasia. It trains, organizes, and equips pro-life leaders around the world to promote and defend the sanctity of human life and the dignity of the family in accordance with the teachings of the Roman Catholic Church. A variety of reports are available on the organization's Web site, and its *FrontLines* newsletter may be ordered from the organization.

International Task Force on Euthanasia and Assisted Suicide
PO Box 760, Steubenville, OH   43952
(740) 282-3810
Web site: www.iaetf.org

Formerly the International Anti-Euthanasia Task Force, the organization opposes euthanasia and assisted suicide. It addresses euthanasia, assisted suicide, and end-of-life issues from a public policy perspective. The goal of the International Task Force is to make certain that a patient's right to receive care and compassion is not replaced by a doctor's right to prescribe poison or administer a lethal injection. The organization's Web site offers an extensive list of resource information.

Justice for All
PO Box 55159, Houston, TX   77255
(713) 935-9300 • fax: (713) 935-9301
e-mail: info@jfa.net
Web site: www.jfa.net

Justice for All is a criminal justice reform organization that supports the death penalty. The organization maintains a Web site database of death row inmates indexed by the names of their victims. The organization's activities include circulating online petitions to keep violent offenders from being paroled.

National Abortion and Reproductive Rights Action League (NARAL)
NARAL Pro-Choice America 1156 Fifteenth St. NW, Suite
    700, Washington, DC   20005
(202) 973-3000 • fax: (202) 973-3096
e-mail: membership@ProChoiceAmerica.org
Web site: www.prochoiceamerica.org

NARAL supports women's right to legal abortion and works to reduce the need for abortions through better access to contraception, health care, and sex education. The organization briefs members of Congress and testifies at hearings on abortion and related issues. Its publications include *Who Decides?*, a state-by-state report on the status of women's reproductive rights, and *Personal Decisions, Personal Responsibilities: Prevention First* to encourage prevention of unwanted pregnancies.

National Hospice and Palliative Care Organization (NHPCO)

1700 Diagonal Rd., Suite 625, Alexandria, VA   22314
(703) 837-1500 • fax: (703) 837-1233
e-mail: nhpco_info@nhpco.org
Web site: www.nhpco.org

NHPCO advocates for the terminally ill and their families. It also develops public and professional educational programs and materials to enhance understanding and availability of hospice and palliative care, convenes meetings and symposia on emerging issues, provides technical informational resources, conducts research, monitors congressional and regulatory activities, and works closely with other organizations that share an interest in end-of-life care. Its new consumer-focused Web site Caring Connections (www.caringinfo.org) provides a wide range of materials about end-of-life care.

National Coalition to Abolish the Death Penalty

920 Pennsylvania Ave. SE, Washington, DC   20003
(202) 543-9577 • fax: (202) 543-7798
e-mail: swisely@ncadp.org
Web site: www.ncadp.org

The National Coalition to Abolish the Death Penalty works with policy makers and their constituencies to adopt legislation in opposition to the death penalty at the local, state, and national levels. It also seeks to expand public information about the death penalty through local and state media outlets and assisting affiliate groups to organize activities in opposition to the death penalty. The organization publishes *Lifelines* newsletter and maintains a variety of fact sheets on its Web site.

National Right to Life Committee (NRLC)

512 Tenth St., NW, Washington, DC   20004
(202) 626-8800
e-mail: NRLC@nrlc.org
Web site: www.nrlc.org

NRLC is one of the largest organizations opposing abortion. The organization's ultimate goal is to restore legal protection to what it calls innocent human life. The primary interest of the NRLC has been the abortion controversy; however, it is also concerned with matters concerning medical ethics, which relate to the right to life issues of euthanasia and infanticide. In addition to maintaining a lobbying presence at the federal level, NRLC serves as an information clearinghouse for its affiliates, the press, and the public. The organization's Web site includes a monthly *NRL News* report along with archives and extensive current legislative information.

Planned Parenthood Federation of America (PPFA)
434 W. Thirty-third St., New York, NY 10001
(212) 541-7800 • fax: (212) 245-1845
e-mail: communications@ppfa.org
Web site: www.plannedparenthood.org

PPFA is a national organization that supports individual rights to make reproductive decisions without government interference. It provides contraception, abortion, and family planning services at clinics throughout the United States. An extensive list of free publications and *Choice Magazine* are available on the organization's Web site.

Bibliography of Books

Jonathan Aurthur   *The Angel and the Dragon: A Father's Search for Answers to His Son's Suicide*. Deerfield, FL: Health Communications, 2002.

Erika Bachiochi   *The Cost of "Choice": Women Evaluate the Impact of Abortion*. San Francisco: Encounter Books, 2004.

Stuart Banner   *The Death Penalty: An American History*. Cambridge, MA: Harvard University Press, 2002.

Hugo Adam Bedau and Paul Cassell, eds.   *Debating the Death Penalty: Should America Have Capital Punishment*. New York: Oxford University Press, 2004.

John Bessler   *Kiss of Death: America's Love Affair with the Death Penalty*. Boston: Northeastern University Press, 2003.

Theresa Burke   *Forbidden Grief: The Unspoken Pain of Abortion*. Springfield, IL: Acorn, 2002.

Leslie Cannold   *The Abortion Myth: Feminism, Morality, and the Hard Choices Women Make*. Hanover, NH: University Press of New England, 2000.

Arthur J. Dyck   *Life's Worth: The Case Against Assisted Suicide*. Grand Rapids, MI: William B. Eerdmans, 2002.

Gloria Feldt   *The War on Choice: The Right-Wing Attack on Women's Rights and How to Fight Back*. New York: Bantam Books, 2004.

Peter Hodgkinson and William A. Schabas, eds. — *Capital Punishment: Strategies for Abolition.* New York: Cambridge University Press, 2004.

Roger G. Hood — *The Death Penalty: A Worldwide Perspective.* New York: Oxford University Press, 2002.

Loretta M. Kopelman and Kenneth A. de Ville, eds. — *Physician-Assisted Suicide: What Are the Issues?* Boston: Kluwer Academic, 2001.

Roger S. Magnusson, with contributions by Peter H. Ballis — *Angels of Death: Exploring the Euthanasia Underground.* Melbourne, Australia: Melbourne University Press, 2002.

James Michael Martinez, William D. Richardson, and D. Brandon Hornsby, eds. — *The Leviathan's Choice: Capital Punishment in the Twenty-first Century.* Lanham, MD: Rowman & Littlefield, 2002.

Georges Minois and Lydia Cochrane — *History of Suicide: Voluntary Death in Western Culture.* Baltimore, MD: Johns Hopkins University Press, 2001.

Helen Prejean — *The Death of Innocents: An Eyewitness Account of Wrongful Executions.* New York: Random House, 2005.

Timothy E. Quill and Margaret P. Battin, eds. — *Physician-Assisted Dying: The Case for Palliative Care and Patient Choice.* Baltimore, MD: Johns Hopkins University Press, 2004.

Christoph Reuter — *My Life Is a Weapon: A Modern History of Suicide Bombing.* Princeton, NJ: Princeton University Press, 2004.

Barry Rosenfeld

Assisted Suicide and the Right to Die: The Interface of Social Science, Public Policy, and Medical Ethics. Washington, DC: American Psychological Association, 2004.

Alexander Sanger

Beyond Choice: Reproductive Freedom in the 21ˢᵗ Century. New York: PublicAffairs, 2004.

Edwin S. Schneidman

Comprehending Suicide: Landmarks in 20th-Century Suicidology. American Psychological Association, 2001.

Susan F. Sharp

Hidden Victims: The Effects of the Death Penalty on Families of the Accused. New Brunswick, NJ: Rutgers University Press, 2005.

Scott Turow

Ultimate Punishment: A Lawyer's Reflections on Dealing with the Death Penalty. New York: Farrar, Straus & Giroux, 2003.

Index

mentally retarded, ban on execution of, 121
Michelmann, H.W., 60
Michigan, fetal protection statute in, 57–58
Mill, John Stuart, 216
"Model State Act to Authorize and Regulate Physician-Assisted Suicide, A," 211–12
moral culpability, of juveniles, 121–22, 124
moral right, physician-assisted suicide is, 214–18
More Guns, Less Crime (Lott), 86
Mother Teresa, 41–42
Muehrer, P., 170
Muhammad, John Allen, 124
murderers
    as deserving death penalty, 16
    juvenile
        should face death penalty, 109–18
        should not face death penalty, 119–28
    repetitive, 80–81
murder rate, affect of executions on, 81–87
Murray, Iain, 79

National Center for Health Statistics, 131, 156
National Health Interview Survey, 147
National Safety Council, 155
National Youth Risk Behavior Survey, 131
Nazis, 60
Neils, Rob, 209
Netherlands
    euthanasia in, 201–3
    physician-assisted suicide in, 211
NRA membership, murder rate and, 85

Nusbaum, M., 162

O'Connor, Sandra Day, 19, 24, 109
Oregon, assisted suicide in. *See* Death with Dignity Act
Ortiz, Adam, 120–21

Page, Susan, 18
pain care, lack of, and physician-assisted suicide, 188–89
palliative care, 195
partial-birth abortions
    do not harm women, 63–68
    pain to fetus during, 42–43, 72–73
    should be banned, 68–74
    statistics on, 66, 73
People v. Kurr, 57
Perry, Rick, 105, 123
personal health, abortion and, 32
personhood, 58
Peterson, Scott, 108
pharmaceutical companies, campaign contributions by, 136
PharMetrics Integrated Outcomes Database, 140
physician-assisted suicide
    abuses in, 200–205
    can be prevented, 206–13
    is a moral right, 214–18
    legitimizes self-destruction, 219–22
    public opinion on, 15, 196
    regulation of, 211–12
    slippery slope of, 209
    violates medical ethics, 182–90
        con, 191–99
    see also Death with Dignity Act
physicians
    oaths taken by, 197–98